The Visible Idea

THE VISIBLE IDEA

Interpretations of Classical Art

by Otto J. Brendel

Art History Series—II
Decatur House Press
Washington, D.C.

Foreword and Translations by Maria Brendel

Typeset by Focus/Typographers, St. Louis, Missouri
Printed by Universal Lithographers, Inc., Cockeysville, Maryland

LIBRARY OF CONGRESS CATALOGING IN PUBLICATION DATA

Brendel, Otto, 1901–1973.
The visible idea.

(Art history series; 2)
Includes index.
1. Art, Classical.   I. Title.
N5610. B73   709'.38   79-25009
ISBN 0-916276-07-4

Decatur House Press, Ltd.
2122 Decatur Place, NW
Washington, D.C. 20008

Contents

For
Christopher and Eliza Foss

Foreword

IN REPUBLISHING A SELECTION of essays by Otto J. Brendel I am realizing a plan my husband developed many years ago. Five were originally published in German and appear here in my translations. Each article deals with the interpretation of an ancient monument and I hope that scholars and students alike will enjoy them and receive answers to some often asked questions.

My very great thanks are due to Professor Frank E. Brown who with valuable comments and advice generously encouraged me. I also wish to offer my cordial thanks to Sharon Dwyer and to all who have assisted in the preparation of the translations. I am indebted to Mr. William M. Voelkle of the Pierpont Morgan Library for most helpful information concerning medieval miniatures. My special thanks to Dr. Hellmut Sichtermann who so kindly aided me in obtaining many photographs from the German Archaeological Institute in Rome.

The articles originally appeared in the following publications: "Procession Personified," *AJA* 49 (1945); "Untersuchungen zur Allegorie des Pompejanischen Totenkopf-Mosaiks," *RömMitt* 49 (1934); "Novus Mercurius," *RömMitt* 50 (1935); "Classical 'Ariels,'" *Studies in Honor of F.W. Shipley, Washington University Studies, New Series, Language and Literature No. 14*, St. Louis (1942); "Der Schild des Achilles," *Die Antike* 12 (1936); "The Hora of Spring," "Dionysiaca," Part II, *RömMitt* 48 (1933); and "Der Grosse Fries in der Villa dei Misteri," *JdI* 81 (1966). I wish to thank the following institutions for granting permission to republish them here: Archaeological Institute of America; Deutsches Archäologisches Institut; Deutsches Archäologisches Institut Rom; Washington University, St. Louis.

Maria Brendel
New York

Figures

Classical "Ariels"

The Shield of Achilles

The Hora of Spring

The Great Frieze in the Villa of the Mysteries

*EPA: Editorial Photocolor Archives
**DAI: Deutsches Archäologisches Institut

Abbreviations

AA	Archäologischer Anzeiger
ABr	P. Arndt-F. Bruckmann, Griechische und Römische Porträts
AdI	Annali dell'Istituto di Corrispondenza Archeologica
AJA	American Journal of Archaeology
AJP	American Journal of Philology
AM	Mitteilungen des Deutschen Archäologischen Instituts, Athenische Abteilung
AntK	Antike Kunst
ArchCl	Archeologia Classica
ArchRW	Archiv für Religionswissenschaft
ArtB	Art Bulletin
ARV	J.D. Beazley, Attic Red-Figure Vase Painters
AZ	Archäologische Zeitung
BCH	Bulletin de correspondance hellénique
BdA	Bolletino d'Arte
BMFA	Bulletin of the Museum of Fine Arts, Boston
BMMA	Bulletin of the Metropolitan Museum of Art, New York
BonnJbb	Bonner Jahrbücher
BWPr	Winckelmannsprogramm der Archäologischen Gesellschaft zu Berlin
CIL	Corpus Inscriptionum Latinarum
CRPetersb	Classical Review Petersburg
CRAI	Comptes rendus de l'Académie des inscriptions et belles lettres
CVA	Corpus Vasorum Antiquorum
DarSag	C. Daremberg-E. Saglio, Dictionnaire des antiquités grecques et romaines (Paris 1877–1919)
EA	Photographische Einzelaufnahmen antiker Skulpturen
FR	A. Furtwängler-R. Reichhold, Griechische Vasenmalerei
GazArchéol	Gazette archéologique
GiornscavPomp	Giornali degli Scavi di Pompeii
HAW	Handbuch der Altertumswissenschaft
HSCP	Harvard Studies in Classical Philology
JdI	Jahrbuch des Deutschen Archäologischen Instituts
JHS	Journal of Hellenic Studies
JRS	Journal of Roman Studies

MAAR	Memoirs of the American Academy in Rome
MdI	Mitteilungen des Deutschen Archäologischen Instituts
MélRome	Mélanges d'archéologie et d'histoire de l'École française de Rome
MemAccLinc	Memorie della R. Accademia Nazionale dei Lincei
MJbb	Münchener Jahrbuch der bildenden Kunst
MonPiot	Monuments et mémoires publ. par l'Academie des inscriptions et belles lettres, Fondation Piot
MythLex	W.H. Roscher, Ausführliches Lexikon der griechischen und römischen Mythologie
NJbb	Neue Jahrbücher für das klassische Altertum
NNG	Nachrichten der Akademie der Wissenschaften in Göttingen
NSc	Notizie degli Scavi di Antichità
ÖJh	Jahreshefte des Österreichischen Archäologischen Instituts in Wien
RA	Revue archéologique
RE	Pauly-Wissowa, Real-Encyclopädie der klassischen Altertumswissenschaft
REA	Revue des études anciennes
RenNap	Rendiconti della R. Accademia di Archeologia, Lettere ed Arti, Naples
RhM	Rheinisches Museum für Philologie
RHR	Revue de l'histoire des religions
RömMitt	Mitteilungen des Deutschen Archäologischen Instituts, Römische Abteilung
RömQ	Römische Quartalschrift
SB	Sitzungsberichte der Akademie der Wissenschaften zu München
SBHeidelberg	Sitzungsberichte der Heidelberger Akademie der Wissenschaften
SteMat	Studi e Materiali di Storia delle Religioni
ZfN	Zeitschrift für Numismatik

The Visible Idea

Fig. 1. Attic Oinochoe, Dionysus and Pompe, New York,
Metropolitan Museum of Art

Procession Personified

A WORK OF UNUSUAL FINENESS, the oinochoe in the Metropolitan Museum with ΠΟΜΠΗ in the middle between Eros and Dionysus, invites close inspection.[1] Questions arise, however, from an examination of its details. Not everything is immediately apparent in this delicate representation (Fig. 1).

First, what is ΠΟΜΠΗ actually doing? At her side stands a splendid specimen of those baskets, "Opferkörbe," which as we well know by now, were used in sundry religious and, especially, wedding rites.[2] It has been suggested that she is decorating the basket.[3] The flaw in this explanation is that she turns away from the very article which we suppose to be the object of her attention. Yet it must be realized that the figure is not represented so as to make the action unequivocal; consequently, there is no simple explanation of it. First of all, however, we should say that she is in the act of dressing. This is how she goes about it. In order to drape herself with the (originally) pink-colored[4] cloak that seems her only garment,[5] she first threw it around her back. In the present, and of course, preliminary condition she keeps it from falling, first, by pushing one part between her knees; second, by holding one of the upper ends with her teeth. The latter is a rather realistic comment by the painter, though not quite as original as it might seem. Examples can be found in other Greek vase-paintings.[6] Yet this attitude demonstrates two things. The figure is represented as dressing, not undressing. With works of art one cannot always say for certain whether a figure is putting on or taking off a cloth, because much the same manipulations are required in order to achieve both—witness the discussion about the Cnidian Aphrodite.[7] But in the present representation the garment cannot slip down because it is firmly, even conspicuously, prevented from doing so: and why should ΠΟΜΠΗ with so much effort hold her mantle if she wanted it to fall? Further, a woman while dressing uses her teeth only when her hands are busy otherwise. The above mentioned vase-paintings show this quite clearly.[8]

Now the lady of the New York pitcher really holds something with both hands, namely, a wreath or garland of gilded leaves; two branches, the leaves of each turned against those of the other, are held together on the top by a golden globule. The fingertips of the right hand are now destroyed, but it seems likely that they, together with the gold branch, grasped another end of the cloak. Logic, as well as the preserved outlines behind the shoulder and the right arm, make this assumption likely. Without some support the cloak would not stay as it is shown in the painting; it would fall back. Consequently, ΠΟΜΠΗ here performs two actions at a time, and both seemed important to the artist so that he did not want to omit either of them.

She dresses and holds the wreath. It is improbable that these occupations merely form two parts of a unified action, that is, the act of getting dressed. The possibility that the wreath too forms part of the lady's attire is remote. She already has a wreath on her head, and where else should such an ornament go? The figures of this style often, because of a pensive lack of determination which is proper to them, create a doubt as to their real intentions.[9] Evidently, in the picture before us, neither the woman nor the god to whom she turns has use for the wreath in her hands. Perhaps she really means to decorate the basket. But at the same time she clothes herself and regards Dionysus who is seated at her left side. These are incongruities, however slight. Yet they are of a kind which is not infrequent in allegorical art and, indeed, in many works they seem designed to catch our attention first. There always are two ways of responding to incongruities. Either we take the patronizing attitude of over-looking them as unessential; or we accept them at their face value as facts laid before us, and seek an adequate understanding of them.

If the latter course is pursued, another question becomes inevitable. The figure ΠΟΜΠΗ, "procession," has been expressly designated by the painter.[10] It is fortunate that he did so; who would recognize her today without the explanatory inscription? The question is, why was a character representing a procession pictured the way it is shown here, as a woman dressing herself? Surely the figure must be regarded as a personification. She cannot be just a participant of the procession,[11] for whom the given action would be even less suitable. Yet it is clear that here one is dealing with a period when the use of personification as a means of pictorial expression was in the formative stage. Later, when a convention concerning personification was established, everything that had a name could be visualized in this manner. In late classical or mediaeval art, it is true that *nomina sunt numina* and as such picturable. In Greek art, the *numina* were there first. Many of them were originally anonymous, generic concepts of the myth-forming imagination, like the maenads and satyrs of Dionysus or the nymphs who, in works of the late fifth and fourth centuries, form the court of Aphrodite. From the ranks of these intrinsically nameless, mythical creatures, Greek art drew its earliest personifications.[12] There are transitional stages, however. The satyr, "Kissos," the sleeping maenad, "Tragodia," on the Oxford oinochoe,[13] remain satyr and maenad and behave accordingly, regardless of their names. But the case of the New York oinochoe is different. ΠΟΜΠΗ there resembles a divine appearance existing in her own right, not merely a part of some conventional, mythical or iconographical pattern. It pays to ask whether her action is not related in fact to the thing for which her name stands. Such a connection is not difficult to find. It may be described as an analogy. A woman arrays herself before making her appearance; likewise, a procession arrays itself or is arranged, before the start. In either case the spectacle promises to be a glamorous one. The personification, if so explained, refers to the preparatory state of a procession when it is about to start. Already she is literally in her boots.[14]

This idea was probably less surprising to the ancient than the modern observer. After all, the Parthenon frieze actually represents the same preparatory actions preceding a procession—in that case, the Panathenaic. The present composition only summarizes these preparations metaphorically, in the image of a woman clothing herself. It is interesting to compare this with the other representation of a ΠΟΜΠΗ in the Metropolitan Museum.[15] She appears in the retinue of Aphrodite. The rather inconspicuous figure quietly displays the necklace which she is about to don. Her attitude is commonplace and the personification, if indeed it may be so called, as yet is little detached from the impersonal types of young women who, in this style, commonly surround and symbolically multiply the charms of Aphrodite. Nevertheless, a convention of how to impersonate the idea "procession," could well be based on such representations. Indeed, it seems already in the making. Already the processional basket is placed beside the personification, like an attribute. One is not forced to understand the occupation with the necklace on this vase as an act of self-adornment, anticipating the dressing scene of the Kertsch oinochoe. Yet one may so interpret it. Moreover, in the latter the figure ΠΟΜΠΗ is at the same time shown as decorating the basket. Now a unified meaning becomes apparent in her two seemingly divergent actions. To array herself, to adorn the ritual implements, are both preparatory acts to the event hinted at. Both constitute suitable, and it seems even traditionally preferred, actions of the lady "Procession."

After this, a third question can be asked and, perhaps, answered. The procession is getting ready. Whence does it set out? Greek art as a rule is rather specific about such matters.

The answer must be sought in the bystanders which we have not so far considered. That is to say, Eros with the elegant wings to the left of the main figure, is not likely to contribute much to this question. The irregular elevation on which he stands must not be called a base; it is a terrain line. Consequently, the figure is not a statue, as is sometimes asserted.[16] His kind is not rare on vases of this period. In numerous compositions one can observe similar characters of secondary importance, though by no means unimportant. They might be called the significant accidentals, a pictorial device that in Greek art deserves a special study. Here it may be pointed out that Eros, natural companion of anything enjoyable, is busy putting on sandals. As he possesses wings and is not forced to walk, this preoccupation with his shoes seems a little ostentatious. The fact is the figure simply parallels and underlines the main action. He, too, gets ready.

Yet Dionysus on the opposite side plays a different role. His presence in this place is very interesting. The rectilinear postament on which his chair is placed is really best explained as a statue base.[17] He is a statue, though we probably must not see in him the actual reproduction of a cult image.[18] He is rather a statue come alive.[19] Or the god in person has taken the place of his temple image. In each case, the point is that Dionysus is comfortably at home, as a god can only be in his own sanctuary. Undoubtedly, this is the god for whom the procession moves out. But his appearance on the elevated base also signifies a locality. And this place is not described as the end of the procession, for the condition of ΠΟΜΠΗ is hardly compatible with a state of arrival. On the contrary, the procession is in a state of preparation or, at most, departure. The reference is to a procession setting out from a temple or precinct of Dionysus.

Everything seems to indicate a specific Athenian institution. It must be doubted that this situation is equally characteristic of all Bacchic festivals in the Attic Calendar. Both the Rural and the "Great" Dionysia were celebrated with *pompae*, but the processions chiefly appear to have moved with their offerings to the sanctuaries, not away from them.[20] Possibly the Lenaea brought a procession through the town, but this is not certain.[21] Nothing recognizably connects the New York pitcher with this feast, anyhow. As to the Anthesteria, we possess considerable information, but it is contained in fragments so dispersed as to make much reconstructing inevitable. Nevertheless, we probably need not separate the Kertsch oinochoe in New York from these materials with which it has been aligned previously.[22] Only in the light of the interpretation here offered, a correction might become necessary.

Our picture has been tentatively brought into relation with the famous *carrus navalis* procession, ascribed to the day of the *Choes*.[23] But does anything in the vase-painting really refer to this event and its characteristic paraphernalia? There are no such references. The situation, as analyzed above, even contradicts the known facts of this celebration, for the same reason that made a relation to the "Great" Dionysia unlikely. The naval car, too, formed like a boat, carries the god to his sanctuary and stresses his arrival, not departure. There is another possibility, however. The rites of the Hieros Gamos did involve a departure when Dionysus, from his residence in the Limnaion, moved to the Bukoleion, which was the appointed place of the symbolical wedding ceremony. It is highly probable, but not certain, that there was a procession on this occasion.[24] Dionysus—his image or the Archon Basileus—had to be transported from one place to the other. The bride, the Basilinna, performed important and mysterious functions in the Limnaion and, consequently, had to be brought to the Bukoleion also. Later, she and perhaps the god too must return to the sanctuary in the marshes; but before that, it was unavoidable that both were carried to the official locality of the wedding rites, which was the Bukoleion. This means that whenever the slightest publicity was given to these movements to and fro of the sacred protagonists of the Gamos, a procession formed almost by itself. This occurred more likely before than after the rites symbolizing the marriage, after the analogy of ordinary wedding customs.[25] A procession from the Limnaion to the Bukoleion, which can, with good reason, be presumed as a part of the yearly Anthesteria, fulfilled the functions of a *pompe* in a very literal sense. It was to escort the god on his way from one to another destination.

Two reasons recommend this explanation for the New York oinochoe. First, it fits the represented situation. ПОМПН is making ready, the preparations occur in the immediate presence of the god, and the god is in his own quarters. He is seated, however, on the same kind of chair as appears on the often-quoted little vase, also in New York, which perhaps renders a childish re-enactment of this very procession.[26] There the chair has already been lifted on the car, and everything is ready for departure.

Second, this interpretation explains the general tenor of the representation. It does justice especially to the specific kind of images used to symbolize the procession in its relation to the god. One should not forget that the woman decking herself out, and

Eros putting on his sandals, as iconographic types belong originally to the gynaeconitis and, especially, to the often-represented wedding scenes. Both evoke the memory of the most common among these scenes, the preparation of the bride. The latter may be dressing herself, or helped by friends and maids, or assisted by fluttering Erotes. The types and their basic significance are well known.[27] Undoubtedly even here, in the different context of the New York oinochoe, the figures of Eros and the dressing lady carry the erotic connotations of their traditional origin. Therefore, they seem very appropriate for an occasion which, like the ΠΟΜΠΗ in question, is also a wedding procession. Iconographically, the figure behaves like a bride, and this underlying parallel may explain why she looks so conspicuously back to Dionysus. In the London oinochoe Dionysus and the seated Basilinna similarly face each other.[28] The present case is different, for ΠΟΜΠΗ is not the bride herself. She only impersonates the procession which is to accompany the god. But while she exchanges with him this glance of mutual understanding, she adds a curiously sentimental and mystic note to the composition.

Notes

1. Inv. no. 25.190. Description and bibliography in G. M. A. Richter and Hall, *Red-Figured Athenian Vases in the Metropolitan Museum of Art* (1936) no. 169, 215f, pls. 164, 177. More recent discussions: K. Schefold, *JdI* 52 (1937) 60; F. Zevi, *Mem. Accad. Lincei* 6 (1938) 355, n. 5; BMMA Guide 1 (1939) 35. I want to express my most cordial thanks to Miss Richter for bibliographical information and photographs, with which she kindly provided me; to Miss Ch. Alexander for her friendly assistance in examining this vase and the other one, mentioned below, Richter and Hall, *op. cit.* no. 160.
2. G. M. A. Richter, *AJA* 22 (1907) 423ff; *AJA* 30 (1926) 422ff; L. Deubner, *JdI* 40 (1925) 210ff.
3. L. Deubner, *Attische Feste* (1932) 103.
4. Richter and Hall, *Red-Fig. Athen. Vases* 216.
5. This appears to be one of the loose garments, himatia, which the women of the Kertsch vases wear quite frequently: see K. Schefold, *Untersuchungen zu den Kertscher Vasen* pl. 7a, woman seated at the right; 7b, standing maenad. A similar cloak fully envelops a companion of Thetis on the pelike from Kamiros, *ibid.* pl. 17 and *FR* pl. 172; another slips back from the shoulders of the women beneath the apple tree on the pelike. Schefold, *Kertscher Vasen* pl. 24b.
6. The pyxis, *Burlington Exhib.* (1904) *l.c.* pl. 100, I 56a, was already quoted in Schefold, *Kertscher Vasen* 105, n. 102. Add: Fragment of pyxis, Tübingen E. 154: J. D. Beazley, *ARV¹* (1942) 537, no. 43; a similar representation. A. Baumeister, *Denkmäler* I 609, fig. 668, after *Gaz. Archéol.* 5 (1879) pl. 23, cf. Beazley, *op. cit.* 663, no. 14.
7. *Gnomon* 16 (1935) 202.
8. Supra n. 6. The women in all these works seem busy binding their belts. The two last named examples show women wearing the peplos; between their teeth they hold one end of the *apoptygma*.
9. A comparable case: lid of a cup in Leningrad; Schefold, *Kertscher Vasen* pl. 14a, girl leaning against a herm. "Der goldene Ölzweig, den die Hände halten, soll wohl ihr eigenes Haar schmücken," *ibid.* 15. This too may be doubted. She already wears a wreath, and there is always the possibility that she will decorate the herm beside her.
10. The letters, originally white, are not recognizable in photographs but can be clearly distinguished when the original is examined closely.
11. In this point I cannot concur with Schefold, *Kertscher Vasen* 14. Cf. Deubner, *Attische Feste* 103, and n. 8.
12. L. Deubner in W. H. Roscher, *MythLex* 3, 2114ff., s.v. "Personifikationen." Cf. similar evolutions in genuine mythical conceptions, like the Moirae; *RömMitt* 51 (1936) 88ff.

13. Beazley, *ARV*[1], 732; oinochoe, manner of the Eretria painter.
14. See description, Richter and Hall, *Red-Fig. Athen. Vases* 215.
15. *Ibid.* no. 160, pls. 159, 176. The legends are in very small letters, but there is no doubt about the reading ПОМПН above the seated young girl with the necklace. Beazley, *op. cit.* 838, no. 46: manner of the Meidias painter.
16. Schefold, *Kertscher Vasen* 14; Deubner, *Attische Feste* 103, n. 5 follows him. Also, it is said that the female figure is a *Kanephoros* representing the entire procession, and distinguished from the gods because she has no base. While a *Kanephoros* might well personify a procession, the one here cannot be human. She is of the same stature as the gods, and in no way distinguished from them.
17. Schefold, *op. cit.* and *JdI* 52 (1937) 60.
18. The objection was correctly raised by G. M. A. Richter, in Richter and Hall, *Red-Fig. Athen. Vases* 215, n. 2.
19. Similar to the statue of Artemis on the Orestes krater at Naples, who seeks to penetrate the darkness of the *adyton,* and therefore protects the eye with her right hand like a person straining her eyes; *FR* pl. 179, and text 363.
20. Deubner, *op. cit.* 140, about the "Great" Dionysia; *ibid.* 138, procession to the temple of Dionysus during the Rural Dionysia as celebrated in the Piraeus. Cf. *ibid.* n. 9, against the suggestion made by E. Buschor, *AM* 53 (1928) 98, n. 1.
21. Deubner, *op. cit.* 125.
22. For a discussion of ancient testimony regarding the Anthesteria, see Deubner, *op. cit.* 93f.
23. *Ibid.* 103.
24. *Ibid.* 105, 109. Cf. M. Bieber, *History of the Greek and Roman Theater* (1939) 96, n. 7; G. W. Elderkin, "The Lenaion, Limnaion and Boukoleion in Athens," *Archaeol. Papers* V 33. The wedding procession of Dionysus and the priestess-queen has already been discussed by A. Mommsen, *Feste der Stadt Athen* 393f.
25. For the procession to the house of the bridegroom, cf. L. Deubner, *JdI* 15 (1900) 149; 51 (1936) 175ff.; A. Brueckner, *AM* 32 (1907) 80ff.; *RE* 16, 2130.
26. Deubner, *Attische Feste* 104f., and pl. xi, 3, 4.
27. Cf. Brueckner, *op. cit.* 79ff.; the material requires re-examination. Figures tying shoes are especially often represented. Either Eros or the bride is so shown, as in Brueckner, *op. cit.* pl. 8, or Eros performs this service for the bride as in *JdI* 11 (1896) 194, no. 46 and Schefold, *Kertscher Vasen* pl. 14a, etc.
28. Deubner, *op. cit.* 101f., pl. x, 1, 2.

Observations on the Allegory of the Pompeian Death's-Head Mosaic

THE DEATH'S-HEAD MOSAIC in the Museo Nazionale, Naples (Fig. 1)[1] is a combination of various mythological and everyday elements the meanings of which are left to the observer to discover. The mosaic, made with great care from small tesserae, consists of a large skull in bony white and gray set in the center of a turquoise blue ground. Apart from the repair along the entire left side, the mosaic is in excellent condition. The main idea of the representation is clear beyond doubt; its allusion to death is obvious. The range of ideas about death, however, is so vast that little is gained by this recognition, and one is left with the task of translating the peculiarities of the allegory into as complete a verbal statement as possible. Three commentators—A. Sogliano, who originally published the mosaic,[2] as well as A. Mau[3] and A. Furtwängler,[4] who later worked on it—tried to fit the mosaic into the area of popular philosophies that recommend trying to enjoy life to the fullest even though death threatens. This old Greek idea expressed in the common motto κτω χρω (take and enjoy) and disguised in the Epicurean *carpe diem* (enjoy the day) was quite widespread, as R. Zahn has shown in a large collection of monuments and literature.[5] That the small mosaic in Naples originally decorated the dining table of a garden triclinium in Pompeii shows how common these reminders of mortality were. It was meant to contrast with the pleasures of eating and drinking, like the famous silver *larva* at Trimalchio's banquet, with the host's comment: *Sic erimus cuncti, postquam nos auferet Orcus* (So we shall all be, after Orcus takes us away).[6] This association as well as the setting and the function of the mosaic must be taken into consideration from the outset in any attempt at an analysis. Since the representation is not immediately self-explanatory, we must see to what extent the composition presents a unified concept.

A wheel, a butterfly,[7] and a skull are arranged in the center of the picture one above the other in a manner that would not be possible in reality. They float weightlessly against the empty ground. The only indication of their physical existence is the little shadow line above the bottom edge. The hidden meaning must be deciphered like a hieroglyph.

Of these symbols, the combination of skull and butterfly is the easiest to understand. The association is almost formulaic and can be found in similar representations on Roman gems[8] and on a bronze weight, once in the Dutuit Collection[9] (Figs. 2, 3). Such objects help to make the meaning clear. The skull and butterfly are not poetic allusions to mortality in general such as one sees everywhere in the Baroque in similar pictures, but rather a reflection—a scientific explanation, as it were—of

Fig. 1. Death's-head mosaic from Pompeii, Naples, Museo Nazionale

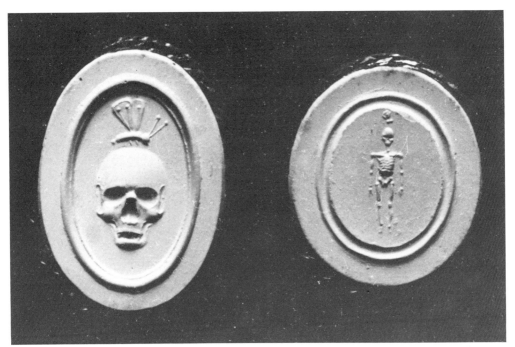

Fig. 2. Roman gems

Fig. 3. Roman bronze weight, formerly
Dutuit Collection

death. Death is represented as Hesychius described it: χωρισμὸς τῆς ψυχῆς ἀπὸ τοῦ σώματος (separation of the soul from the body).[10] From the time of Heraclitus, this is the most common formula for its philosophical definition.[11] Death is the separation of body from soul, an impersonal conception. Hesychius in his gloss also clearly separated this formulation from the actual god of death, Thanatos. The elements are also separated in images where the butterfly sits on the skeleton or crawls over the bare skull, as if it were a recently abandoned chrysalis. The image of death is made accessible by identifying skull and bones as nothing more than the lifeless and soulless remains of the body. The pictorial usage is familiar enough from the above-mentioned representations of the ΚΤΩ ΧΡΩ where the dead bones have exactly the same meaning; they serve as a responsory, as it were, to the aphorism "take and enjoy" by providing the obvious reminder: "as long as there is time."[12] One is in the midst of an eminently rational world of ideas. All these works do without a pictorial image of the mythical Thanatos in favor of what one might call an analytic representation of death. It is here in the realm of popular skepticism that the image of a skeleton slips into Greek pictorial thought as an allusion to death; it is a realm totally alien to the mythical-poetic world ruled over by a god of death and the underworld, who is represented in the beautiful pictures on Attic white lekythoi,[13] and who walks across the stage at the beginning of Euripides' *Alcestis.*[14] It is highly characteristic that the drunken Herakles, in his big scene in the same play, repeatedly voices the motto of the *carpe diem* and seems to be almost unaware of the personified Thanatos. His goddess of death is Tyche, whose position as such was consolidated in the course of time. These are the same wisdoms that Petronius' Trimalchio later enunciates over his little silver skeleton.[15] In this realm skeleton and skull become conspicuous pieces of evidence in an irrefutable *argumentum ad hominem.* They are hieroglyphic signs employed from the start to set forth an entirely non-mythical, practical-moral sequence of thought, and on this rests the peculiar readability common to all of these inventions.[16]

The second element of this curious symbol is the butterfly. Its meaning and frequent use as the image of the fluttering soul is well known.[17] It is more natural to find it sitting on top of the skull as in gems or on the Dutuit bronze weight; the mosaicist though was perhaps forced to put the butterfly underneath for the sake of the composition, for the pendulum, as we shall later see, had to rest above the skull. It is possible that this alteration represents a reflection such as the one in Marcus Aurelius IV, 41.[18] We may safely attribute a degree of conceptual flexibility to these symbols, even though they are put together rather schematically. Thus one of the most noteworthy variants of the "skeleton with butterfly" figure appears on one of the silver cups from Boscoreale.[19] Its *larvae* are variously occupied, and one of them grasps a butterfly's wings with the fingertips of its bony left hand. The figure is inscribed ψυχίον, little soul, employing a diminutive ending just as the Marcus Aurelius passage does.[20] According to H. de Villefosse, the skeleton offers the little soul to his neighbor, an explanation which is neither clear nor convincing, because the neighbor pays no attention to it; he is far too occupied with bestowing a wreath and with conducting his rickety orchestra. Furthermore, the little soul is moving in another direction, struggling mightily, but with no success, to reach its tormentor's other hand which holds up a well-filled moneybag. The inscription over the bag reads φϑόνοι, envy, which brings to mind another image. On a Berlin gem Eros holds the tormented soul in exactly the same manner as he playfully singes it with the burning torch;[21] he too tortures the poor butterfly, just as the malicious skeleton on the Boscoreale cup does; but, our peculiar pamphleteer makes it clear that it is not the fire of love that burns so fiercely. Envy, the φϑόνοι, is quite sufficient to make a soul fidget in pain. A trend toward irony clearly underlies such inventions.[22]

In the mosaic, the wheel adds little that is new to the main subject, death as the separation of body and soul. It is a kind of "basso continuo" accentuating the given notes, being as it is an attribute of both Nemesis and Tyche. In the strict sense of the word it is an ominous sign and is meant to bring to mind the inevitable close of the whole train of thought,[23] which in its transparency is all important for the composition. So far we are in agreement with the earlier interpretations of the mosaic; the skull is still the most important element of the picture. However, the path to understanding now leads in a different direction and takes an unexpected turn.

Around the central group there is a frame-like construction vaguely resembling an *aedicula* with a pointed gable. This whole misleading assemblage gives a certain impression of architectonic order when in fact it too lacks any corporeal static reality. As before we are dealing with an almost rebus-like combination. The construction consists of two supports, the one on the right, as has earlier been recognized, is a *pedum* or shepherd's crook, the gnarled and bent end of which is easily identifiable. A bag hangs from the stub of a branch just below the curve in the *pedum*, the lower part of which is covered with a cloth fastened by a string knotted in a bow. The bag and *pedum* are no real problems, as their association is known; we find the same sort of bag hanging from a cut branch on a *pedum* beside the statuette of Diogenes which W. Amelung reconstructed.[24] The strange tassels that dangle from the two corners of the bag as from an old powder sack are even more distinct in the marble. The meaning of these objects is clear, as it was shown by Amelung. They are the πήρα, the knapsack and *pedum*, which were for Diogenes the indispensable accouterments of the philosopher's wandering life. The oddly disheveled traveler in one of the Farnesina landscapes[25] is similarly equipped, as he carries on a conversation with a woman. And like a still life, the *pedum* with the goatherd's tied-up leather sack is among the rustic Bacchic objects of the offerings on the so-called Ptolemy Cup.[26] The circle to which these objects belong is clear: they are the possessions of peasants and shepherds, of tramps and mendicant philosophers.[27] They are the possessions of those who need nothing, and of the poor.

For this reason it is difficult to follow Sogliano's interpretation of them as "beni terreni di cui la morte ne priva";[28] instead, a better case may be made for interpreting them as earthly tribulations. It is reasonable to assume that this is also what the mosaicist had in mind. In any case, he combined a natural and human interpretation with a reflection that becomes easily understood if one takes into consideration the other side of the picture. For there, as a pendant to the *pedum*, is an object unquestionably suitable to stand for the height of wordly goods and human power: a scepter. The identification is beyond question. To confirm it we may refer to the well-known coins of T. Carisius from the troubled years around 45 B.C. on which the new power of Caesar presents itself with symbols of the world rule[29] which, in addition to the cornucopia, celestial sphere, and rudder, include the scepter.[30] On the coins (Fig. 4) the scepter is shaped exactly like the one in the mosaic. This narrow staff ends in a point like the *sauroter* of a spear, and at the top there is a spherical knob set between two horizontal discs correspondingly rendered on the coins down to the last detail. That is what the scepter to which Caesar aspired looked like. In the mosaic, around this symbol of sovereignty there is wound the other sign that proved so fatal for him: the ribbon that hangs fluttering from the scepter is certainly no ordinary white ribbon, but the diadem. One recognizes it by the fringes so carefully depicted on both ends.[31] Thus Mau must have been correct in interpreting the piece of red cloth, which becomes the third attribute, as a length of the purple.[32] How different it is from the coarse and tattered rag on the other side has been clearly shown. Thus the scepter, the purple, and the diadem are symbols of a king just as on the opposite side the *pedum* and the knapsack are those of a beggar.

This conclusion is crucial to understanding the whole picture, for it enables us to establish within the framing elements of power and poverty a definite sphere of ideas into which the reference to death is inserted. At the same time we encounter here, consciously rendered, one of the basic elements of an allegory: the contrasting pair. The pair of king and beggar, the most legendary and popular of all social antagonism, furnishes the logical prerequisite of the idea represented. For a specific idea is intended, rather than a common play on the symbols of death; this can no longer be doubted. A composition of ideas is emerging just as in a Hellenistic epigram, and only the last of its signs, connecting the contrasting pair like a lintel, remains to be deciphered. It is obvious that the actual point of the epigram that has been transformed into a rebus lies there.

The connecting element, placed as such over the picture, is a large, carefully drawn carpenter's level. One corner rests on the scepter, the other on the *pedum*. It has the visual shape of an open angle, its edges carefully covered with metal, corresponding to the capital letter A in the Latin alphabet. A plumb, a small metal cone, hangs from the top of the angle on a string, point down and resting on the skull. This tool, called *libella* in Latin, is a leveling instrument belonging to builders and architects. It serves a purpose similar to the hydrostatic level.[33] We know its use from the relief from Delos that shows two craftmen erecting a stone altar (Fig. 5).[34] According to H. Blümner, "if the surface on which it is set is exactly horizontal, the string will align with the center of the crossbeam; if not, the surface is uneven and must be adjusted."[35] That is its normal use, and the one to which it is put in the Naples mosaic. However, here it is not an ordinary surface on which the level rests, but rather on a scepter, the symbol of royalty, on one side, and on a beggar's *pedum* on the other. The plumb line hangs conspicuously straight despite these differences, stressing the complete equality of the objects being measured. By this simple expedient the picture becomes intelligible at its most decisive point. What is measured or established by the level is in Latin called *aequalitas*; the activity itself is *aequare*.

Fig. 4. Coin of T. Carisius

Fig. 5. Votive relief from Delos, Mykonos Museum

Aequalitas is the point here, that is to say the *aequalitas* of such unequal things as the fates of a king and a beggar. The contrasting pair, the sum total of all human differences represented by their outward appearances, fits thereby into a closed, logical structure, so that the picture's allegory becomes immediately comparable to the structure of a spoken phrase. *Mors*, death, is its subject, *aequare* its verb. At last, when one finds the sentence thus phrased in a verse of Claudian, *Omnia mors aequat* (Death makes all things equal),[36] one may claim to have found a literal translation for the Pompeian mosaic.

One hardly has the impression that this phrase, which in the end sifted so naturally out of a picture as rich in associations as this, contains anything startling or strange. Quite the opposite is true. It is a matter of a self-explanatory, proverb-like reflection. But it is the first example that leads back to the world of popular moralizing ideas to which this special class of images of death refers time and again. Once more it is confirmed that this kind of memento mori is wholly unmythical, but includes instead a practical reference to this world and to everyday life. Thus it argues with its logic against human hubris. Horace's "Ode to Q. Dellius" presents a collection of all these thoughts, a suitable drinking song to such strange images: the meaning and composition of the famous lines 21ff. correspond almost completely to the mosaic:

> *Divesne prisco natus ab Inacho*
> *nil interest an pauper et infima*
> *de gente sub divo moreris*
> *victima nil miserantis Orci;*
>
> *Omnes eodem cogimur omnium*
> *versatur urna . . .*

(Whether thou be rich and sprung from ancient Inachus, or dwell beneath the canopy of heaven poor and of lowly birth, it makes no difference: thou art pitiless Orcus' victim. We are all being gathered to one and the same fold. The lot of every one of us is tossing about in the urn. *Carmina* II. 3.)

The name of Inachus, the earliest Argive king, has the same connotation as the scepter. The poem conveys not only the idea of the final equality of all human beings but, as in the mosaic, it does so by establishing a pair of social contrasts.[37] Only the image of death is significantly different. While the poet mentions the urn and pitiless Orcus with a new poetic consciousness, we perceive in the cruder symbols of the mosaic a glimmer of the popular origin of all those concepts. Among their many forerunners none comes as close as the satire of the Cynics.[38] There too the skull is quite properly pivotal when, for example, Lucian confronts Diogenes, the mendicant philosopher, with the once powerful satrap Mausolus without nose and eyes and with teeth bared.[39] This is the line of reasoning behind the Cynics' diatribe, one of their special applications of the old proverb Γνῶθι σαυτόν (know yourself).[40] How precisely it was understood in this circle is illustrated by the well-known mosaic in the Museo Nazionale delle Terme in Rome (Fig. 6);[41] from such a background emerges their warning against the vanity of human differences that can only be accidental and transitory. From the moral precepts of the Cynics this idea spreads like a subterranean current, unexpectedly and often emerging in a variety of places. It links up with the portentous metaphor of the *mimus vitae*, which probably also goes back to the Cynics,[42] thence becoming a brick in the intellectual architecture of the Early Christian sermon.[43] In a slightly different form, but with the same solemnity, it appears in the emperor Marcus Aurelius' historical meditation: Ἀλέξανδρος ὁ Μακεδὼν καὶ ὁ ὀρεωκόμος αὐτοῦ ἀποθανόντες εἰς ταὐτὸ κατέστησαν (Death reduced to the same condition Alexander the Macedonian and his muleteer).[44] Its modern history in the satire of the medieval Dance of Death created by the guilds is well known; its development there took place very much as it had in antiquity, proceeding from the sermons of the mendicant friars to symbolic representations of the power of death.[45] The beginning of modern poetry abounds in meditations of this kind.[46] Thus, ever-flowering antiquity creates before our eyes the spiritual forces that are destined to survive it by centuries.

The Naples mosaic, though only a modest utilitarian object for its Pompeian owner, finds its natural historical place and literal interpretation in this significant connection. For this reason alone it seems unlikely that such a relatively isolated monument was the only one that communicated the ubiquitous idea. The bridge connecting the anonymous mosaicist with the larger world of his evocative imagery must have been an established pictorial tradition. That this is the case is confirmed by a beautiful gem, unfortunately somewhat damaged, in the Thorwaldsen Museum, Copenhagen (Fig. 7).[47] There is nothing now to stand in the way of its interpretation. Again there is a skull in the center of the composition. We can assume that wheel and butterfly were underneath, where the gem is broken off. The level with its plumb hanging is clearly shown above the skull, as is the sack hanging from a stick. The long staff that crosses the *pedum* has been called a thyrsus but in fact it must be the scepter and the diadem. Thus, the meaning of the whole may again be translated into the sentence: Death makes kings and beggars equal. What the Pompeian mosaicist was employing, therefore, was only a popular allegory. The rebus of death which makes all equal was a common device during Late Hellenism and at the beginning of the Roman Empire.

Now one may venture to introduce the remarkable etching by Borioni, in which an ancient gem, now lost, is preserved (Fig. 8).[48] Here, various symbols, some of them known, others new, are united to form an apparently mysterious whole. In spite of its appearance, there is sufficient reason to examine the odd invention and not to condemn it out of hand as a Baroque forgery. Although there are more objects, the arrangement corresponds to the other monuments we have seen. Instead of the skull, we have an entire skeleton in the center. The level, with the straight plumb line hanging over the skull, and the wheel are present, but the latter object has become an unsteady footstool. The skeleton sits atop an ordinary amphora such as

Fig. 6. Roman mosaic, Rome, Museo Nazionale delle Terme

Fig. 7. Roman gem, Copenhagen, Thorwaldsen Museum

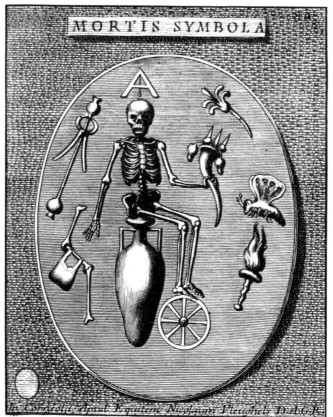

Fig. 8. Lost Roman gem

was commonly used to contain wine and oil, and also for burials. A surprise is the cornucopia in the skeleton's left hand, perhaps filled with poppy capsules, but the details of the etching are hardly reliable. With much more confidence, however, we meet again the familiar butterfly at the right, fluttering over a burning torch. As on the Boscoreale cup, the torch can probably be interpreted as ζωή (life).[49] A flower is placed above, so that one finds a collection of symbols signifying life on this side of the gem. On the opposite side, the usual sack appears. But from what is it hanging? Ignorance and the minuteness of the original representation must have caused a misunderstanding on the part of the draughtsman who drew the three strangely joined bones, for the sack, after all, belongs with the *pedum*. In total perplexity about the scepter and diadem, known to us from the Naples mosaic, the etcher also improvised the abstruse structure above. Thus, in spite of these mistakes, it is not too difficult to guess what was on the ancient gem. It was based on the concepts found on the other works discussed here, apparently adopting mainly the symbols and the composition. But in adding other similar images to the combination, the gem lost the precise coherence of the original idea and in the end it offers mere signs instead of a striking allegory. The level no longer measures the beggar's *pedum* and the king's scepter; it appears here without any logical connection, its origin being intelligible only to the knowing. In the sense of a modern allegory, the decisive step was taken towards making the hieroglyph independent.[50]

An etching by Sebald Beham (Fig. 9) may connect the end of this essay with its beginning.[51] It belongs here on account of its title, *Mors omnia aequat*, which is a variation of the verse by Claudian. However, the actual preciseness of the old idea has been completely abandoned. The almost physically established equality of king and beggar is replaced by a more general interpretation of human evanescence: the object becomes the bearer of poetical meanings, and a new poetic sentiment is heralded in the reflections on death.[52] But it is not our purpose here to follow its journey into the emotional world of the Baroque and of Romanticism.

Notes

1. Naples, National Museum 871 (109982), meas. 0.45x0.50 m. Cf. excavation report by A. Sogliano, *Giornscav. Pomp.* 3 (1874) 9.
2. Sogliano, *ibid.*
3. A. Mau, *Pompeji in Leben und Kunst* (Leipzig, 1900)[2] 417ff.
4. A. Furtwängler, *Die Antiken Gemmen* (Leipzig, Berlin, 1900) III 298. A correct interpretation of the level is given in E. Caetani-Lovatelli, *Thanatos* 44 and W. Déonna, *BCH* 56 (1932) 463f. with a poor drawing taken from S. Reinach, *Répertoire des peintures grecques et romaines* (Paris, 1922) 267, no. 14, in which the other objects in the picture are unrecognizable.
5. *Catal. Berl. Mus.* 35 (1914) 296 and ΚΤΩ ΧΡΩ, 81, *Berl. Winckelm. Prog.* (1923) 9ff. See also E. Preuner, *JdI* 39 (1925) 48ff.; for the epitaph of Sardanapalus, F. Dornseiff, *Hermes* 64 (1929) 270f.
6. Petronius, *Satyricon* 34.
7. The wings are red with blue dots, Sogliano (supra n. 1). The body appears in the background.
8. Furtwängler (supra n. 4) pls. 29, 48; for similar representations, *MythLex* 3235, s.v. "Psyche."
9. *Catal. Froehner* (1897) pl. 43.
10. Hesychius, *Lexicon*, s.v. "θάνατος."

Fig. 9. Sebald Beham, etching, Mors omnia aequat, Rome, Gabinetto delle Stampe

11. E. Benz, *Das Todesproblem in der stoischen Philosophie* (Berlin, 1905) 10, 3. Cf. W. Altmann, *Die röm. Grabaltäre d. Kaiserzeit* 179, no. 173.

12. R. Zahn (supra n. 5).

13. E. Buschor, *MJbb* N.F. 2 (1925) 174ff.

14. L. Weber, *Euripides Alkestis* 21ff.

15. Zahn (supra n. 5) 10. Lessing already recognized the importance of this passage for the interpretation of pictures of skeletons, *"Wie die Alten den Tod gebildet,"* *Sämtl. Schriften*, ed. Lachmann-Muncker (Berlin, 1838–40) 11, 47. Under the same title supplement by J.G. von Herder with important ideas about the relationship of mythical to allegorical concepts, cf. J. Kont, *RA* 24 (1894) 13. Furthermore it is clear that from these moralizing reflections on death the skeleton passed from ancient art into Christian allegories in the familiar form of the grim reaper.

16. Cf. the carved gem that Zahn (supra n. 5) convincingly interpreted with the aid of a Hellenistic epigram.

17. See O. Waser, *MythLex* 3234, s.v. "Psyche," for the ambiguity of the word Psyche; also *ArchRW* 16 (1913) 382ff., *JHS* 45 (1925) 62ff. For etymological contributions to the symbolism of the butterfly, O. Immisch, *Glotta* 6 (1914) 193ff. The concept is widely known even in Chinese: *CR Petersb.* (1877) 34, 58ff.

18. Ψυχάριον εἶ, (βαστάζον) νεκρόν, ὡς Ἐπίκτητος ἔλεγεν (Thou art a little soul bearing up a corpse, as Epictetus said).

19. A. H. de Villefosse, "Le Trésor de Boscoreale," *MonPiot* 5 (1899) pl. 8, 2, far left; text 59ff. and 234. Cf. M. I. Rostovtzeff, *Gesellsch. u. Wirtsch.* (Leipzig, 1929) I 210.

20. Likewise "animula, vagula," etc., in verses by the Emperor Hadrian, O. Immisch, *NJbb* 18 (1915) 201ff., cf. *RhM* 71 (1916) 406ff.

21. Cf. the gem, Berlin 1639.

22. Same combination of φϑόνοι and skull on the other cup (supra n. 19). Goethe commented twice on the sarcastic meaning of ancient pictures of skeletons, *Dichtung u. Wahrheit*, Weimar edition 27, 165 and *Der Tänzerin Grab*, *Schriften zur Kunst* 48, 146f.

23. The wheel of Tyche moves swift and unrelenting: B. Schweitzer, *JdI* 46 (1931) 181. Cf. *Anacreontea*, ed. K. Preisendanz 32, where the life cycle is compared with the wheel of a moving carriage and the invitation to enjoy life is added.

24. *AJA* 31 (1927) 287ff.; contra G. M. A. Richter, *Metrop. Mus. Stud.* 2 (1929) 39. For the identification, see R. Eisler, *RA* 33 (1931) 1, 5ff.

25. P. Marconi, *Pittura dei Rom.* fig. 114.

26. E. Babelon, *Camées de la Bibl. Nat.* 368, pl. 43. Cf. old peasant at a "watering place for cattle," in the Vatican Mus.: T. Schreiber, *Hell. Rel. Bild.* pl. 74.

27. Diogenes, the cynic, calls people "without *pera*" cripple, *Diogen. Laert.* VI. 33; the propaganda was successful so that stick and bag soon could be added to the image of the philosopher; later they belonged to the picture of early monkhood. We can trace here also the equipment of the sarcastic, preaching Cynics to the cup with skeletons from Boscoreale. The inscriptions introduce the two philosophers among the busy *larvae* on the cup as Zeno and Epicurus, both founders of their schools, see Amelung, *AJA* 31 (1927) pl. 8, 1. They are involved in a debate the result of which seems to be conditioned by their bony nature. The thesis is stated in the inscription "τὸ τέλος ἡδονή"; cf. Villefosse (supra n. 19) 61ff., 228f. The "supreme good" is clearly indicated by the round cake which Epicurus, accompanied by the proverbial little pig, is enjoying while Zeno is arguing. This amusing scene could have been taken from a collection of jokes of the Cynics, e.g. from a Diogenes anecdote such as the one in *Diog. Laert.* VI.56; cf. the fragm. *Philos.grec.*, ed. Mullachius, II 317, no. 191 with a parallel phrase or the answer by Demonax, Lucian, *Dem.* 52. This is quite important for the comprehension of the cups with skeletons, cf. Zahn (supra n. 5) 8. From the doctrines of the Cynics the joke about the cake was transferred to the debate of the two philosophers, just as the dress of poverty which actually does not belong to them; it is regarded, however, as the philosophers' costume. Moreover, the Epicureans claimed the cake for themselves already in Lucian's "Fisher," *Piscator* 43. It is clear that all these pictures of skeletons are based on an unmythical, scientific idea of death; their purpose is satyrical: the struggling little soul in the hand of the skeleton and the quarrel about the cake of the dead philosophers are definitely satirical ideas, that is, in the sense of the Cynics; they all serve the new radicalism of moral conduct which at this point makes itself strongly felt in ancient life. Hence they are part of a universal satire of human life. By referring to the inevitability of death

these ideas express the most effective criticism of the follies of the living.

28. Sogliano (supra n. 1); also Mau (supra n. 3) where the significance of the *pera* is more correctly assessed.

29. H. A. Grueber, *Coins Rom. Rep.* (London, 1910) III pl. 52, 4–6 and I 528. The same scepter appears on coins of Juba, *ZfN* 28 (1910) pl. 1, 1 and 16.

30. For the interpretation of these coins and their political allegory, A. Alföldi, *Hermes* 65 (1930) 369ff. The epigram from Philae, *ibid.* 370 goes perhaps somewhat further. Its concept of the world-ruler on earth, on the sea, and in heaven obviously appears again in Vergil's acclamation of Augustus, *Georg.* I. 24ff. and in G. Wissowa's passage of Aratus, *Hermes* 52 (1917) 103. The coin with the celestial sphere and the rudder which are easily understandable is based on the same program. Alföldi also claims the scepter for the sovereignty over countries. Here too we are dealing with the triple rule which is crowned by the cornucopia as symbol of good fortune.

31. Cf. Alföldi, *ibid.* 371 and the Egyptian coin with double cornucopia and diadem (Fig. 10).

32. Alföldi, *ibid.* 418. The cloth tied around the scepter is red with dark shadows and white highlights. The coarse cloth tied to the *pedum* is shown in "shabby" shades of grayish white on dull yellow; it could be linen or perhaps wool. Cf. the rhetorical comparison by Fronto, *Fronto ad M. Antoninum de eloquentia*, ed. Naber 144: *Fac te, Caesar, ad sapientiam Cleanthis aut Zenonis posse pertingere, ingratiis tamen tibi purpureum pallium erit sumendum, non pallium philosophorum soloci lana.* Courtesy, A. Alföldi.

33. Representations of the *libella* are common, esp. on tombstones. H. Blümner, *Technologie* (Leipzig, Berlin, 1912) 3, 91, fig. 2; A. H. de Villefosse, *MémAntFrance* 62 (1901) 205ff.; *MélRome* 32 (1912) 110, fig. 12. H. Gummerus, *Jdl* 28 (1913) 63, 105, 113ff. F. Frigerio, *RivArchComo* (1933) 70 shows that the *libella* was an Egyptian invention, called Daedalic by the Greeks; *ibid.* 115, fig. 40, fragment of a sarcophagus, discovered by M. Gütschow in the Praetextat catacomb. See Déonna, *BCH* 56 (1932) 425ff. for the large collection of material up to the Middle Ages.

34. *Ibid.* pl. 27 and description, 421ff. On a ceiling picture in the Palazzo Zuccari, Rome, a level is shown being used in the same way as in the ancient relief (Fig. 11). The photograph was kindly provided by the Biblioteca Hertziana.

35. Supra n. 33, 2, 235.

36. *De raptu Proserpinae* II. 302.

37. The confronting of the king with the beggar is quite typical, even in Horace, *Carmina* I.4.13ff. *Mors aequo pulsat pede pauperum tabernas, regumque turres* and likewise in the Ode to Postumus, *Carmina* II.14.11f., *sive reges sive inopes erimus coloni*.

38. It goes back at least as far as Homer, cf. Achilles' bitter speech about the indiscriminate end of all mortals, *Iliad* IX. 318ff.

39. Lucian, *Dialogues of the Dead* 24; cf. C. Helm, *Lucian and Menipp.* 199.

40. Menippus maliciously sings these words to the kings Croesus, Midas, and Sardanapalus, who are lamenting their fate in the underworld, Lucian, *ibid.* 2.

41. R. Paribeni, *Museo Naz. Romano* (1932) 64, no. 57. Cf. E. Caetani-Lovatelli, *Thanatos* 49 shows that this picture from a tomb on the Via Appia did not serve as the common exhortation to enjoy life. The point is actually the slogan of the Cynics, cf. Helm, *ibid.* 198. Likewise in a tomb epigram from Antium, emphasized by the representation of a skeleton, J.Geffcken, *Kynika und Verwandtes* 3. From here the path leads to the portrait of Hans Burgkmair and his wife, Vienna, Kunsthistorisches Museum (Fig. 12) by Lucas Furtenagel, in which two skulls stare out of the mirror at the two thoughtful viewers, with the inscription "Erken dich selbs"; this is not only the ancient motto, but it is also used in the connotation of the Cynics which concerns us here. We do not know how the same mirror of self-examination with the skull that answers questions came into the hands of a Chinese Taoist monk in the mid-18th century, see Tsao Hsueh-Chin, *The Dream of the Red Chamber*.

42. U. von Wilamowitz-Moellendorf, *Hermes* 21 (1886) 626 in reference to the last words of Augustus; E. Petersen, ΕΙΣ ΘΕΟΣ 257. Hence the picture is also related to the motto of the Cynics on the Boscoreale cup, *MonPiot* 5 (1899) 61, σκηνὴ ὁ βίος. In reference to Shakespeare, *As You Like It*, Act II.7.140, "All the world's a stage," cf. F. Boll, *Njbb* (1913) 131ff. and 134. For typical contrasting pairs in this context, see Helm (supra n. 39) 53.

43. St. John Chrysostom I. 780 B ff., together with an illusion to "the day when the masks come off." Cf. H. Reich, *Der Mimus* (Berlin, 1903) I 197.

44. Marcus Aurelius, *Meditations* VI. 24, trans. C. R. Haines (1916). For Marcus Aurelius' pessimistic

Fig. 10. Alexandrian coin

Fig. 11. Federico Zuccari, ceiling painting, Rome, Biblioteca Hertziana

Fig. 12. Lucas Furtnenagel, Portrait of Hans Burgkmair and his Wife,
Vienna, Kunsthistorisches Museum

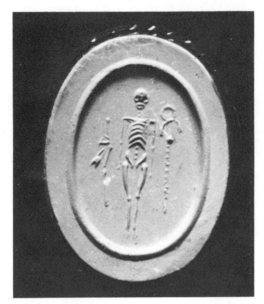

Fig. 13. Roman gem

Fig. 14. Allegorical figure

philosophy of history, see Benz, *Das Todesproblem* 65. Medieval poetry took up the same historical examples of transience, e.g. Alexander and Caesar in Friar Lamprecht, see W. Rehm, *Der Todesgedanke in der deutschen Dichtung* 30 and similar ideas in *Der Ackermann aus Böhmen, ibid.* 128, Benz, *ibid.* 127; Burdach, *Kommentar* 264.

45. For the origin of the Dance of Death: E. Mâle, *L'art religieux de la fin du moyen age* 362.
46. Petrarca, *Trionfo della Morte* 79ff.:

> Ivi eran quei che fur detti felici
> Pontefici, regnanti ed imperatori;
> Or sono ignudi, poveri e mendici . . .

F. von Logau (17th cent.), a new version of the old theme:

> Schlaf und Tod, der macht Vergleich
> Zwischen Arm und zwischen Reich,
> Zwischen Fürst und Bauer . . .

For more, similar examples see F. P. Weber, *Aspects of Death* 283ff.
Likewise Goethe, Weimar edition, V.1.154:

> Geburt und Tod betrachtet' ich
> Und wollte das Leben vergessen;
> Ich armer Teufel konnte mich
> Mit einem König messen.

47. Katal. Fossing 1639; from a cast, courtesy Thorwaldsen Museum. The Leningrad gem, mentioned by Treu, *De ossium humanarum imag.* 21, no. 55 probably belongs here too (Fig. 13). The level is missing, perhaps owing to the gemcutter's ignorance; Cades IV, E, 67.
48. Borioni, *Collectanea antiquitatum Roman.*, Rome (1736) pl. 80. G. Treu, *ibid.* 37, no. 107. Déonna (supra n. 33) from a later, incomplete drawing. It is unconvincing that the verse from Cicero, *De div.* II, 4, 5 with the mistake "perhibeto" instead of "perhibebo" was actually on the ancient gem, Borioni, *ibid.* 56.
49. *MonPiot* (supra n. 19) 61.
50. For the survival of the level as symbol of *aequalitas* see Déonna (supra n. 33) 468ff. In C. Ripa's *Iconologia* the level occurs several times in this sense, esp. in later editions (e.g. Siena [1613] II, 112) in the hand of a man as "Ordine dritto, giusto" (Fig. 14). F. von Bezold, *Fortleben der ant. Götter* 59, from a medieval verse from *Metamorphosis Goliae Episcopi*:

> an plus valeat Pallas Aphrodite
> adhuc est sub pendulo,
> adhuc est sub lite.

51. A. von Bartsch, *Peintr. Grav.* 28. The engraving (Gabinetto delle Stampe, Rome) has been reproduced several times, not on account of its simple meaning but because it was of such high quality.
52. For the whole problem, see G. Fricke, *Die Bildlichkeit in der Dichtung des A. Gryphius* 118ff.

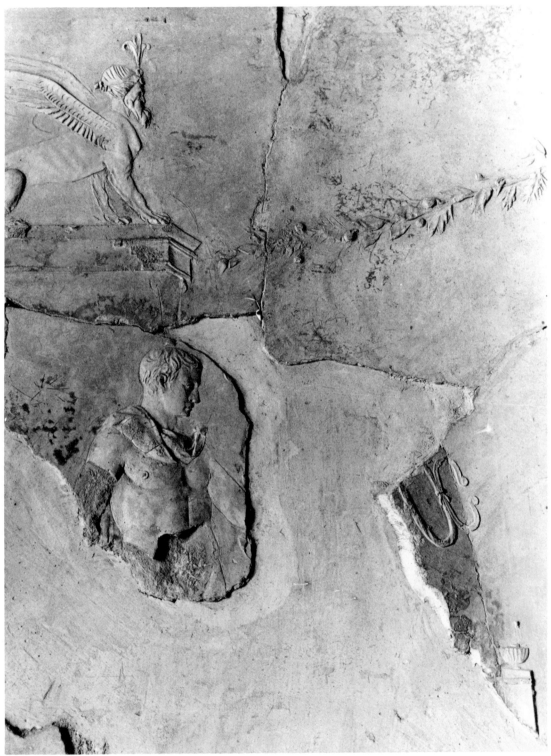

Fig. 1. Ceiling from the Villa Farnesina, Rome, detail, Rome, Museo Nazionale delle Terme

Novus Mercurius

I. State Of Preservation

THE STUCCO FRAGMENT in Figure 1 found its correct place finally in the reconstructed barrel vault of the Farnesina.[1] From the connection with a beautiful caduceus on the other side of the break we can infer that the fragment contains the upper part of a figure of Hermes. Considering the debate of K. Scott about the equation of Augustus and Hermes, the figure deserves careful inspection. It is not an ordinary Mercurius.

Where else in Roman-Hellenistic art would Hermes have such distinguishing features (Fig. 2)? One would expect a low, energetic forehead, a wreath of upward curling hair, a short athletic nose, and full lips.[2] What we see here is, however, something quite different. For a work with a purely decorative purpose the head is very carefully executed. It is shown in sharp profile, which was popular on Augustan reliefs, and the precisely drawn outline of the noble head is as clear cut as the image on a coin. Long curving locks are indicated in seeming disarray falling onto the forehead, but closer examination reveals order in the disorder. The hair is parted above the right temple; some locks sweep to the right joining others that fall straight from the middle of the forehead. A third group falls in a double wave from the top of the head where it is just barely noticeable to end in a crescent next to the ear. The forehead itself is straight, its uneven surface ending in hollow temples; a smooth eyebrow curves above the downward gazing eye. The delicate nose is unusually long, and a strong chin accentuates the lower half of the face. In spite of a slight damage at its edge, the energetic silhouette of the lean cheek can be easily followed.

E.L. Wadsworth has already pointed out that these features can only belong to a portrait and we certainly share her impression that it resembles portraits of the Claudian family.[3] Thus the number of possibilities is limited. Of the known portraits of the new dynasty only one, that of its founder, can be seriously considered, all the more since the later members cannot, on chronological grounds, appear on a monument the style of which corresponds with the final stage of the second Pompeian style. Comparison with established portraits of Augustus such as the one in the Uffizi in Florence (Fig. 3) shows that the choice of Augustus is correct; he is even about the same age as the Mercury on the Farnesina fragment. This juxtaposition needs no further comment; the main parts, the hair and profiles, correspond to each other as well as can be expected in works of such different kinds and purposes. The sharp, eagle-like bridge of the nose shown in the marble portrait is less pronounced on the

Fig. 2. Ceiling from the Villa Farnesina, Rome, detail, Rome, Museo Nazionale delle Terme

Fig. 3. Portrait of Augustus, Florence, Galleria degli Uffizi

Fig. 4. Gold medallion, Este, Museo Nazionale
Archeologico

fragment, yet it is still noticeable. In the iconography of Augustus it was no longer uncommon for individual features of the portrait to follow an idealizing general design. Likewise the splendid gold medallion from Este (Fig. 4), takes the form of a profile directly comparable with that of the Mercury on the stucco fragment.[4] It is also worth noting that the head in Florence belongs to those[5] that show the youth with the sprouting beard as the mourning son of Caesar, a type which became influential especially in the 30s B.C.[6] The head of the stucco fragment is beardless and therefore no longer demonstrates this argument, but it belongs on account of the arrangement of the hair to the same series, as a latter offshoot. In any case we include it with the Bologna altar[7] and the gem with a caduceus as a new representation of the emperor as the god Hermes.

II. COMMENTARY

This rather simple account necessitates the more difficult task of an interpretation. We can refer to existing studies without listing and investigating again the known information relating to Hermes-Augustus,[8] but we must attempt to find out what we can learn from this new discovery. How does the fragment relate to the rest of the stucco ceiling? It is surprising that this new Mercury is only a small, unaccentuated part of a large ceiling composition. Thus, it belongs to an apparently fantastic, ornamental, and therefore alogical structure which teems with inventions and attracts by allusions without communicating any special meaning.

The system of the ceiling. The question is whether such a composition calls for a commentary at all. Its decorative purpose is immediately obvious. However, the formal structure of the overall composition requires as much study as the content.[9] A. Mau has given us a description of the ornamental plan which is very useful as a means of orientation.[10] According to him the ceiling, a barrel vault, belongs to Room 2.[11] It consists chiefly of the two parallel sections at the lower sides, which form transitions down to the wall; above, in the four corners, are squares decorated with grotesque faces in star-like frames. There is finally the center piece which is composed of various motifs in the form of a dodecagon; in between are frieze-like strips. Thus the formal order results from a symmetric correspondence of the various parts. These parts are areas which, when enclosed by frames, can be regarded as pictures. A stream of delicate plant ornaments flows around them as if they were islands bringing forth not only blossoms but also human beings, winged girls, and fabulous animals. The plants are of an ornamental fancy which one can also find elsewhere, artificial forms that have no likeness to real vegetation, but rather resemble the wondrous capriccios of a glassblower.[12] Two pictures with definitely objective representations which correspond to each other emerge from these ornamental meanderings. They are located in a special place in the middle of the two lower sections. E. Petersen was the first to see their relationship to the myth of Phaethon.[13] On one, Phaethon makes the fatal request before the throne of his father who is identified as the sun-god as well as a charioteer.[14] He is accompanied by old Kyknos who, as his pedagogue, carries his sword for him. The corresponding picture shows the Horae preparing the sun-chariot.[15] Because of these principal pieces the room could be called the room of Apollo: *Tuus iam regnat Apollo* (Your own Apollo is now ruler). Yet the emblems remain formally isolated here as elsewhere in similar decorative systems. If any relationship exists between them beyond the frame, the correlation of the Phaethon pictures would indicate where to look for it: the analogy with regard to content follows the formal law of the symmetric arrangement. Therefore, we must be sceptical about Petersen's "sun-wheels" in spite of the presence of Apollo. The fact that four of these structures are above the outer pictures of the bottom section proves their ornamental character; four suns just do not exist. They are in reality *gorgoneia*, certainly shown in a strange and new stylistic fashion, but their origin is recognizable. We have only to trace back the vegetal scrolls to see that their forms were based on the octagonal scale-aegis such as the one on the Late Caesarian coin of Rufus.[16] Before the Baroque allegories one could hardly call this decorative invention a sun adorned with its rays.[17] Consequently we must also drop Petersen's suggestion to extend the sun symbolism to the long outer pictures of the bottom tiers. A double frame separates them clearly from the middle emblems which evidently differ from them with regard to composition and the height of their figures.[18] Moreover the images cannot represent the palace of Helios since no palace can be discovered in them. They are, however, connected to each other by the symmetric arrangement of the whole composition in which they occupy the four corners. The correspondence of the location continues in the compositions of the four panels, the preservation of which permits us to see that they all follow the same scheme. It can be easily described.

In each case the same light architectural structure appears on the right and on the left. Thus, symmetry continues in the individual pictures. On each side, supporting the entablature, is a statue characterized by its attributes as an image of a god. The statues appear twice on each picture. Furthermore, they are not only completely alike, but they face each other like reflections in a mirror. On the entablature above their heads two sphinxes and two griffins are perched in a corresponding manner. Delicate festoons hang down like a curtain from the middle of the upper frame toward the architectural structures to the right and left. As from the garlands in the house of Livia, rustic implements including two shepherds' flutes hang from where the garlands are attached. An idyllic landscape protected by the attributes of the gods is between them. This scheme is repeated four times with small variations; its playfulness is thus multiplied in the whole composition, antiphon and harmony become evenly effective, and the picture itself, constructed of typical elements, appears as carrier of an ingenious if only formal counterpoint. However, part of the rules of this symmetry is that the content be analogous to the external scheme whereby it becomes itself part of the design. Correspondences are not absent here either and become evident by the fact that though they differ from each other in a few obvious details, the four corner pictures are composed in the same manner. But they are not mere repetitions. Rather the images are structures of a special kind, like verses in a poem. It is most important that in each case a different deity rules, personified in double heraldic statues. Three of them can still be identified: Zeus with the eagle, Demeter with sheaves of grain, and Hermes with a lowered caduceus.

Statue of a god and a portrait. The fragment with the head, which is fortunately well enough preserved so that we can recognize the decisive features of the young Augustus, is part of the corner picture with Hermes.[19] As in the other corner pictures the statue is shown twice, and presumably the one that is missing was the same since the beautiful caduceus belonging to it exists to this day. By being incorporated into concrete architectural structures the figures are both equally bound to the unreality of the place which contains the surprising motif of the transformation of the god.

The statue itself is essentially an image of a god, not that of an emperor, just as in the other areas.[20] Yet the portrait confers on it a special attribute whereby it becomes Novus Mercurius.[21] The transformation is visible only in the profile, the face proper. The lines of the neck and the back of the head do not belong to the portrait but allude to well-known aspects of the Hermes statue.[22] The famous words of Horace are thereby represented: *Sive mutata iuvenem figura ales in terris imitaris* (Changing thy form, thou assumest on earth the guise of man, *Carmina* I. 2. 41 ff.). The picture reveals the multifaceted chiasmata of these words; the "winged-one" sets foot upon the earth and as a reminiscence only a symbolic wing of the caduceus remains. The transformation of the figure, though, is confined to the face; Hermes is always *iuvenis*, but the lively features of the well-known countenance transform him into a human youth. So far the image can be directly interpreted by the poem. It is not the deified human being that is the subject here, for the god has assumed the features of the emperor.[23] The god descends into the world that is in need of order; he allows himself to be called by human names, *Caesaris Ultor*, *Pater* and *Princeps*, or finally *Dux* and *Caesar*. In the picture the portrait is decisive; in the poem, the name.

These strange ideas which culminate in the ode by Horace together with the Augustus-Hermes from the Farnesina, can be dated approximately at the time of the battle of Actium.[24] They are part of a long series of expectations of the appearance of the savior of the world, most of which had indeed preceded these manifestations by several years.[25] The Farnesina fragment seems to depend also on a portrait of a relatively youthful Augustus even though the stucco relief itself could hardly have originated during the hero's early years.[26] Many portraits have in common a peculiar familiarity with the features of the youthful emperor, when he was still regarded more as one to be hoped for than as one who had proven himself. His real looks and real face have been held in higher esteem in these surroundings than that of any other human image after him. The shepherds in Vergil's first Eclogue speak proudly of having seen him;[27] his countenance will forever exist in their hearts.[28] Legendary dreams, one of which was transmitted even under the name of Cicero, refer to the appearance of the boy whom the dreamer recognizes in real life with amazement as the fulfiller of the prophecies.[29] "More pleasant runs the day when like spring his face has beamed upon it."[30] One could speak of a general adoration for the image of the youth who assures these hopes, and which the artist of the Farnesina ceiling has meaningfully identified with his Novus Mercurius.

The architecture. It is surprising that the artist combined the portrait of the young

Augustus with a statue which he fitted as a telamon into a small ornamental architecture according to the plan that was discussed earlier. This would be very strange if it had been meant to be a real likeness; however that is hardly possible. Like the duplication of the statue, the architecture is a decorative idea executed exactly the same on all preserved corner panels. Consequently the Mercury shares his fate as a playfully invented telamon with the other corresponding images of gods. The idea, however, though it is abstract, remains noteworthy. It does not necessarily belong to the architectural landscapes among which M.I. Rostovtzeff had placed the Farnesina picture.[31] We can argue with greater reason that the architecture itself is typical of, or at least that it is derived from, still recognizable typical motifs. The well preserved corner of the Zeus panel shows the situation best.[32] An architecture that serves some purpose is out of the question because there is neither wall nor building but only two epistyles which meet at right angles in the middle on a pillar in such a way that the front leg appears in its entire length while the other seems to be seen in perspective. Moreover the head of the front beam rests on one of the forementioned statues; the beam at the rear on a bearded herm.[33] What purpose does such a structure serve? The only answer to this question is indicated by the metal vases with high handles on the epistyle in the background and by an *oscillum* which hangs from the epistyle in front; these vases are votives and the beams which carry them are what Rostovtzeff has called the sacred gate.[34] We are dealing with a repetition of the motif in so far as now two sacred gates meeting at a right angle seem to form a new building which in reality is simply the combination of two well-known ones.

Yet all this does not explain why statues of gods which are emphasized by bases and herms replace the usual pillars. The reference by Mau-Lessing to similar inventions at the top of the painted walls leads only to the observation that the motif was common at least in the Farnesina.[35] However, there are no images of gods; if they were used at that time we still have to discover them. But what gave the stucco craftsman, no matter how inventive he was, the idea of substituting gods and goddesses for caryatids and atlantes? E. Paribeni has been able to cite two heads found in the Tiber, Apollo and Dionysus, which were used in the same way.[36] Two more heads in the Museo Torlonia (Figs. 5, 6), which can also be traced to an architectural use, are even more revealing.[37] A modius on top of each head forms the transition to the architecture as in the case of those in the Museo Nazionale delle Terme in Rome; it is perhaps justifiable for the bearded head which has locks of hair covering its forehead as the figure obviously represents the god Sarapis. His female companion with an elephant skin over her head and the horns of a cow like the goddess Isis is a good match for him. We recognize in her the common image of Africa.[38] Two things follow from this: on the head of the Mercury from the Farnesina there rises a calyx-like form with turned down volutes at the top. The gods in the corresponding panel show the same form. Obviously it is the calathus which regularly carries out the transition from the human to the architectural form; only it has become unusually slender and flowery according to the rule of proliferation which is in general one of the rules of ornamentation. Moreover, the heads in the Museo Torlonia give a first hint at the origin of the inclusion of images of deities into an architecture, the use of

Fig. 5. Sarapis, Rome, Museo Torlonia

Fig. 6. Africa, Rome, Museo Torlonia

which hardly developed within the Greek world. Africa and Sarapis are characteristic Egyptian-Alexandrian figures and must be evaluated as an Egyptianizing element wherever they appear in the architecture of a Roman villa.[39] The same seems to hold true for the gods who support epistyles in the Farnesina, for Egyptian ideas are still remembered in the figure of a winged sphinx who crouches on top of the epistyle (Fig.1).

Sphinxes by themselves would certainly be too common a motif at the time of Augustus to be decisive for such a statement.[40] The history of the emperor's own signet shows, however, that under no circumstances should they be treated as insignificant. Several authors have testified that at the beginning of his career Augustus sealed with a sphinx;[41] the image still appears on the Pergamene coin of the year 20 B.C., and on the armor of Primaporta.[42] Thus, a change took place only after this period because, according to Pliny, the symbol was too ambiguous, a circumstance which however might have been welcome to the emperor at the beginning of his reign. Apart from her atropaic power which was appropriate on the armor as well as on the ring, the sphinx has been of old the sibylline animal and was accepted as such in the sign language of early Augustan coins.[43] Apart from being the proper crest for the predicted ruler of the world she was also the royal animal in Egypt, enough of a hint for the knowing.[44] When Augustus, after 20 B.C., gave up the sphinx as his seal to replace her by the portrait of Alexander the Great, he unveiled somewhat his intentions and he defined them exactly in line with the plans that he had already introduced.[45] He substituted a religious-political model for one of religious speculation. As a result his own likeness followed on the last seal which he used; having reached the end of his life, he has become himself. His successors also took over, together with his title, the seal with his portrait, thus acknowledging his exemplary importance.

Therefore a special symbolism would be evident in the image of the sphinx in connection to a completely personal statement about the emperor. The bearded Farnesina sphinx, however, belongs to the casual world of the ornamentation. Nevertheless we should notice some formal pecularities which distinguish him from so many others, for instance the archaizing hair style and especially the headdress in the shape of a trifoliate blossom, a kind of tiger lily. He is comparable to the bearded male sphinx with a headdress, one of a pair of sphinxes on a fanciful Campana plaque in the Vatican Museo Gregoriano, which flanks a female half-figure carrying the sistrum of Isis.[46] This is another Egyptianizing association and as such the non-Greek beard and headdress are characteristic. The strange sphinx and the use of statues of gods as telamons on the ceiling of the Farnesina should be likewise interpreted. They are Egyptianizing elements of the kind that occur also in the third style in Pompeii.[47] They are very cleverly used here in order to fit the meaningful images, subtly as it were, into the decorative scheme with its architectural structures repeated eight times. Nevertheless we should remember here that, as R. Reitzenstein has demonstrated, the redeeming god from heaven, he whom Horace expected in the figure of Mercurius Augustus, probably had been an idea which had originated in Egyptian religious thought.[48] Once more is the reference to form confirmed by content. It is not by accident that we encounter the son of Maia with the features of the new ruler of the world in these surroundings.

Interpretation. The figure of Augustus-Hermes is essentially different from the one on the Bologna altar in figure and in bearing, as well as in its placement and purpose. There Mercury, hurrying along, wisely counseled by Minerva, and carrying the auspicious money bag which everybody wants for himself, is a well-known Italic figure. The message is obvious and was probably clearly understood. The new ruler was expected to be a god of fortune bringing prosperity in the same way as the Mercurius Augustus found on numerous votive inscriptions.[49] The added portrait of the sovereign turns into an allusion of hope. There is a good deal of indication, as K. Scott has noted, that the image and the expectation was viewed in that way by the Augustan colleges of the priests of Mercury.

Part of the caduceus of the corresponding figure in the Farnesina is preserved, but there is no trace of any other attributes. The still recognizable left wrist with the mantle wrapped around it makes it unlikely that the hand held a purse. The hat and winged shoes are also missing. The lack of attributes may be characteristic for the classicistic stance which keeps allusions to a minimum, but this peculiarity also distinguishes the figure from the two similar ones quoted above. It belongs to another world, and is mainly related to another work which is in some ways also hard to interpret, the statue by Kleomenes in the Louvre (Figs. 7, 8). The classicism of this excellent work needs no explanation; its model is known.[50] Furthermore, it is important that the statue does not represent the Roman Mercury, the god of commerce. It defines the god quite differently, as *Logios*, and that concept is combined with a Roman portrait. For reasons to be discussed later it is, however, quite possible that this work too is a representation of the emperor himself. The oratorical gesture[51] which was probably taken over from the model, and which is so significant for this figure, belongs first of all to the god and only then to the human who became a god by transformation. The gesture is indicative of a wiser Mercurius than the profane one had been; the turtle creeping from under his mantle reminds us of his taste for the arts and of his invention of the lyre. Considering the selection of these qualities we find a type that is quite different from the one to which we are accustomed, and the addition of an individual human face is all the more conspicuous. Thus it was that the people from Lystra greeted the miracle working apostle as the descended god Hermes,"ἐπειδὴ αὐτὸς ἦν ἡγούμενος τοῦ λόγου."(because he was the chief speaker)[52]

To remember these facts is of interest here, because they refer to a sphere of meanings which contemporaries already recognized as Egyptian. *Dicitur* (sc. Mercurius) *in Aegyptum profugisse atque Aegyptiis leges et litteras tradidisse; hunc Aegyptii Thot apellant* (It is said that he [sc. Mercurius] fled to Egypt and handed over laws and the alphabet to the Egyptians; ever since the Egyptians call him Thot).[53] *Logios* and *Nous* are identical with the Egyptian Hermes-Thot to whose descent Horace related the name of the new Caesar. Again image and poem meet. No other known monument approximated in the same manner Horace's conception of Mercurius-Augustus.[54] They meet again in the same magic space that the Farnesina ceiling seems to open up. Both appear to be directly moved by the same ideas and concepts;

both have appropriated, as it were, a mystical Egyptian component.[55] The correspondence seems to be complete.

Here finally Hermes becomes *Basileus Soter* as he had been for the Pharaohs and the Greek Ptolemies.[56] Does this mean, however, that he must be completely set apart from the simpler and less solemn Mercury of the Italic citizen? It almost seems so. Not only the contradictory pictorial concepts but also the strangeness of the expectance of divine grace by which Horace hails him suggest such a conclusion.[57] But the general spiritual tone of the time is to reconcile tensions and to welcome, as confirmation, originally foreign notions. Horace himself has erected a very strange monument for his contradictory god, *superis deorum gratus et imis* (welcome alike to gods above and those below, *Carmina* I. 10. 20), starting the description again with the *Logios* but then falling back upon popular concepts. Since it is known that Horace as *vates* called himself *vir Mercurialis* we must look in such circles for the place where the opposing elements actually merged.[58] In both layers of the concept the point in question is the happiness of mankind; only the ethical content of its argument was different.

Just as Horace addresses in his poem four deities of atonement, Apollo, Venus, Mars, and Mercury, the Augustus of the Farnesina ceiling belongs together with four gods all of whom protect their blessed territories in the way described by Horace. The territories, though individually somewhat different, are always a combination of the typical elements which Rostovtzeff has described.[59] The selection itself is noteworthy; still recognizable are sanctuaries, peasants making offerings, and grazing herds. We can only allude in passing to the wide range of ideas that each of these pictures reveals, because they themselves seem to have sprung from a dreamlike reminiscence rather than from real knowledge. *Tua Caesar aetas fruges et agris rettulit uberes* (Thy age, O Caesar, has restored to farms their plenteous crops, *Carmina* IV. 15) is already a more transparent reference wherein, as in Vergil, the blessings of the earth are named as the primary gifts of the golden age, "Thy age, O Caesar."[60] In such a landscape men perform the pious works of their serene life, they are the *pia gens* of the poets, the untroubled human race in a reconciled world.[61] Yet here meaning that can be interpreted retreats into the intertwining decorative pattern out of which it appeared. No further interpretation of the delicate picture which shows in equal parts playfulness, faith, and poetry, can be offered.

III. THE SO-CALLED GERMANICUS

Thanks to its quality the Kleomenes statue in the Louvre (Figs. 7, 8) is excellent evidence for the transformation of the god Hermes into a portrait of a Roman personality. This work by a Greek artist, a combination of a portrait and the statue of a god, is exactly analogous to the transformation of the Augustus-Hermes of the Farnesina ceiling. The change is confined to the face, otherwise the statue is a replica of the classical one.[62] The formal process is obvious; of greater importance is the change of meaning in the figure which exceeds by far a mere classicistic caprice. The

Fig. 7. Head of a statue by Kleomenes,
Paris, Louvre

Fig. 8. Head of a statue by Kleomenes,
Paris, Louvre

Fig. 9. Portrait of Augustus, Rome, Museo
Capitolino

Fig. 10. Portrait of Augustus, Rome, Museo
Capitolino

question about the identity of this humanized *Logios* must be asked not only with regard to iconography but also with regard to content and history.[63]

The face is unfortunately reworked. Following are some remarks by L. Curtius about the condition of the statue: "The old oval base is set into the modern rectangular one; thumb and forefinger of left hand, right foot and cranium are also new. The face is badly cleaned." J.P. Six was right in assuming that the upper part of the head, now restored to fit the ancient cut, takes the place of an originally separate piece which may have been a petasus.[64] The outfit of the statue would therefore have corresponded also in this detail to the classical model. The modern reworking of nose and mouth makes it difficult to judge the features of the face. F. Studniczka's suggestion, however, to equate the head with that of the Barracco medallion is contested by the basic difference in proportion between the upper part of the head and the lower half of the face, one with a dominating, projected forehead, the other with an energetic, forward thrusted chin. Exactly these qualities, which belong to the general construction of the head, can hardly be affected by a superficial reworking. Stylistically both this portrait and the Farnesina portrait are indeed very similar; the concise forms, so rich in realistic observations, emphasize in both the same gloomy and meditative, almost morose mood. This expression is known from Augustus portraits of the years between 35 and 25 B.C.[65] The statue by Kleomenes must be dated during the same early Augustan period, which means it is contemporary with the poem by Horace.

If one goes back for a physiognomical comparison to the head in the Capitoline Museum (Figs. 9, 10) it seems striking that the general construction of face and skull of the figure in the Louvre resembles Augustus much more than the relief head in the Barracco Museum, especially when a petasus originally brought out the wide upper part of the head. They have in common also an expression of intellectual tension produced by an unmistakable lifting of the left eyebrow, an involuntary manifestation, as it were, while all other features are perfectly controlled. Nevertheless, some differences should be mentioned, mainly in the way the hair falls over the forehead. Instead of the interlocking hair, the locks of "Germanicus" fall naturally, slightly to the right. The established Augustus portrait has a somewhat more pointed chin, smaller round eyes, and a smaller mouth; unfortunately it is there and at the tip of the nose that the reworking makes itself felt. All the same we must ask if the Kleomenes statue represents a personality who may not be known to us.

For this question it is important, considering the style of the portrait and the form of the letters of the inscription, that the possible dating of the statue be restricted to a rather narrow period, hardly extending beyond the reign of the Emperor Augustus.[66] For that period, even in the cult of the dead, all examples of such a monumental equation of humans with Mercurius are missing.[67] The statue in the Vatican (Fig. 11) which first comes to mind has a head equipped with the wings of Hermes, but it shows clearly the characteristics of the Flavian portrait style.[68] A figure in Mantua confers the same deification to its youthful hero, but it dates from the time of Commodus.[69]

Scott has collected more evidence that the equation between god and human being

Fig. 11. Deceased man as Mercury, Rome, Musei Vaticani

lies outside this area.[70] For the apocryphal story of Simon Magus, O. Weinreich cited two more cases, both from the time of the Empire and from the Greek East where similar overstatements had occurred already in Hellenistic times, e.g. Menekrates' *thiasos* of the twelve gods shows Nikagoras from Zelea as Hermes.[71] The idea is definitely not early Roman. When Augustus imitated Alexander by taking up certain of his table manners the reason for doing so was to emphasize the idea of the cult of the ruler,[72] the concept, with regard to its origin and claim, going beyond the purely religious and into the sphere of the private man. However, the late republic, which expressed everywhere its expectations of the new emperor of the world, took surprising liberties with regard to manifestations of the idea—and not only at the height of the struggle for power.[73] Cicero, in his malicious self-defense against the reproach for having styled himself as Jupiter and his sister as Minerva, left a strange testimony.[74] These ideas were so common at that time that they called for a recantation; they were obviously perceived as an aberration or sacrilege. However, were such things still possible after Augustus prevailed in his struggle for power? The proclamations for the deification of Pompey, Mark Antony, and even of Brutus precede of course the battle of Actium. Thereupon such proclamations become a privilege of the victor until they begin to disappear altogether as contradictions to Roman religion. Where they survive, they are limited to the private sector, like the Trimalchio episode, to be ridiculed finally as caprices. With the spread of the emperor-cult a connection between the Italic Mercurial Collegia and the Augustalia developed in many places.[75] Consequently Augustus can appear as the Roman Mercury on the Bologna altar but an unknown person could not have done so.[76] The supersession of the idea of leadership by the idea of sovereignty which A. Alföldi has discussed had been carried out in the meantime.[77] Under these circumstances the Kleomenes statue will have to be accepted indeed as a representation of Augustus in spite of some pecularities. It is a unique work and the deviations from the customary portrait of the emperor might be explained by the deliberate intent of the artist; the portrait is less precise but not obliterated. Nonetheless he, and no one else, is the Novus Mercurius of the decade of Actium.[78]

Finally a strange Roman ring stone, the reference of which I owe again to Curtius, must be considered in this context. It was sold as an image of Mercury at the Vente Drouot, 21 November 1913 (Coll. Comtesse R. de Bearn);[79] its whereabouts has been unknown ever since. The identification was based on the winged caduceus behind the right shoulder of the man represented, which is the characteristic arrangement on coins and gems.[80] In the same way the modern stone in New York, whose portrait conspicuously resembles the medallion in the Museo Barracco, probably took the addition of a turtle and herald's staff from a good ancient model.[81] However, whereas the New York portrait, which is provided with the same mercurial objects as the Kleomenes statue, is not recognizable on the copy, the Drouot gem can be more clearly defined. Hermes who is nude except for a bit of mantle on the left shoulder is certainly a portrait, most likely one of Augustus. For comparison we must turn this time to quite a different series of portraits and mainly to the small bronze bust in the Louvre with the dedication by a certain Atespatus.[82] The art historical analysis of that portrait cannot be developed here, but I agree with P. Marconi's attempt to attribute it to a series of representations of the emperor which must be dated later than the statue of Primaporta. It is significant that in this group of works indications of the emperor's age are not infrequent, and that, in addition, the typical arrangement of the Augustan locks parted above the forehead has given way to another that was not so traditional. This is where the Drouot intaglio belongs. In this way the sad, contracted eyebrows and the free arrangement of the forelocks which are not copied from the Primaporta head can be explained on a face that otherwise has the features of Augustus. Basically the situation is the same as in the small bronze bust, except that the hair hangs somewhat deeper onto the forehead and the right outer group of locks is pushed into the locks in the middle, whereas the opposite is usually the case. But the differences are not sufficient to transform an unknown contemporary of the emperor into Mercury against all probability and evidence; by virtue of Mercury's far-reaching and mysterious significance, Augustus himself had appeared as this god.

Notes

1. E. Paribeni, *Museo Nazionale Romano* (1932) no. 493. It is not yet mentioned by A. Mau-J. Lessing, *Wand-und Deckenschmuck eines Röm. Hauses* pl. 13, but was correctly placed by K. Ronczewski, *Gewölbeschmuck* pl. 11a. Cf. E. Petersen, *RömMitt* 10 (1895) 72. The matching breaks prove that the fragment belongs in this place.
2. The Mercury of Rennes, *GazArch* I (1875) pl. 36, seems to have all this and is therefore not Augustus; cf. K. Scott, *Hermes* 63 (1928) 21ff. The statuette in Cologne, *Pantheon* 14 (1934) 377, represents the same common type, only the mantle and wings are different.
3. *MAAR* 4 (1924) 26.
4. S.L. Cesano, *Atti e Mem. d. Ist. Ital. Numism.* 8 (1934) 104ff. I wish to thank the author who kindly provided the cast which M. Felbermeyer used for the photograph.
5. Type B, cf. O. Brendel, *Iconographie des Augustus* diss. Nuremberg (1931) 65; for date, 37ff.
6. For interpretation and dating of the beard (supra n. 5) 38ff.
7. K. Lehmann-Hartleben, *RömMitt* 42 (1927) 163ff. His identification of the portrait of Augustus is confirmed by Scott (supra n. 2).
8. Lehmann-Hartleben, *ibid.* Scott (supra n. 2) 15ff. Also E. Bickel, *BonnJbb* 133 (1928) 13ff. I wish to thank Scott for the following reference: K. Kerenyi, *De teletis Mercurialibus observationes* II, *Philol. Közlöny* 47 (1923) 150ff. A. Alföldi, *RömMitt* 50 (1935) 106.
9. Complete composition Mau-Lessing (supra n. 1) pl. 12/13.
10. Mau-Lessing, *ibid.* 13f.
11. *Ibid.* 6, with illustration of ground plan.
12. Mau has referred to the quite similar inventions in the so-called *ala sinistra* of the Palatine house (supra n. 1). A. Ippel, *Der dritte Stil* 38f., lists connections with Campana reliefs.
13. *RömMitt* 10 (1895) 67ff. P. Hartwig, *Philologus* 58 (1899) 481ff. W. Helbig and W. Amelung, *Führer durch Rom³* 2, 117. C. Robert, *Sarkophagreliefs* 3, 3, 407ff.
14. Cf. the Primaporta armor, *RömMitt* 25 (1910) 31.
15. Petersen (supra n. 1). Also Robert (supra n. 13).
16. B. Grueber, *Coins Rom. Rep.* 3, pl. 51, 15. The form can be traced to a Hellenistic one which is known from the Tazza Farnese, A. Furtwängler, *Gemmen* 3, 54. H. von Rohden and H. Winnefeld, *Architekt. Röm. Tonreliefs* text 223, fig. 4532, for interesting transition to the Farnesina "suns" on terracotta plaques, where the meaning of the *gorgoneion* is retained. Cf. the *gorgoneion* with similar ornaments on the Arch of the Cavii in Verona, A. Avena, *L'arco dei Cavii* 9.
17. For instance on the breast of Prudentia in the allegory of virtue; cf. the symbol of the *Roi Soleil.*

Bernini's *Truth Unveiled by Time* holds such a form as the sun who "brings it to light"; M. von Boehn, *L. Bernini* 41. Cf. *BdA* 29 (1935) 273.

18. The reason for this difference is probably that the two Phaeton pictures reproduce well-known pictorial compositions, as E. Gabrici has shown on the relief with Horae from Bolsena, cf. Robert (supra n. 16). The other pictures of the Farnesina ceiling are newly invented.

19. Complete illustration *MAAR* (supra n. 3) pl. 3.

20. The lower half of the figure of Hermes can be completed according to the mirror image. A classical posture is obviously attempted, even more so in the figure of Zeus, including the head, *MAAR* (supra n. 3) pls. 5, 1. The way in which classical motifs of statues is used is typically Neo-Attic similar to those on bases of candelabras, as, for instance J. Caskey, *Boston Catal.* 101, or. Pal. d. Conservatori, Galleria 81.

21. For the use of this originally non-Roman name, Kerenyi (supra n. 8) 160, 62.

22. The unmistakably straight back of Augustus's head looked quite different, as all marble portraits testify, including the one supra n. 5. Coins sometimes show similar variations, for instance H. A. Grueber, *Coins Rom. Emp.* pl. 118, 3. The same holds for the gem with *kerykeion*, Lehmann-Hartleben (supra n. 7).

23. R. Reitzenstein, *Poimandres* 176ff. The Pauline theology also presupposes a physical transformation when Christ assumes the form of a servant, *Philippians* 2. 7. Nevertheless, man can also turn into the image of the god in hermetic ideas, cf. Reitzenstein, *ibid.* 21, *Gebet* 3, 11. Likewise Calpurnius, *Bucol.* 4. 142ff. referring to Nero and literally imitating Horace: *Tu quoque mutata seu Jupiter ipse figura, Caesar, ades seu quis superum sub imagine falsa Mortalique lates.* E. Bickerman, *ArchRW* 27 (1929) 25.

24. For its date see A. Kiessling-Heinze, *Kommentar* 10f.; probably the winter of 28 B.C.

25. Compilation of literature by F. Sauter, *D. Röm. Kaiserkult in Martial und Statius* 7ff. Interesting for the historical sequence are the coins of between 45 and 30 A.D. See especially A. Alföldi, *Hermes* 65 (1930) 369ff.

26. The precise date of the Farnesina House is not yet certain. Ippel, *D. dritte Stil* 41, reminded us of the villa where Cleopatra is said to have stayed; yet this attribution which implies a building, at least of the time of Caesar, is incompatible with the existence of a portrait of Augustus in its decorations. The masonry, *tufa opus reticulatum*, cf. Mau (supra n. 1) 5, does not offer enough evidence for a precise date. The pictures and decorations are somewhat more significant. They belong to the last phase of the so-called second style, cf. Mau-Lessing, *ibid*; C. Wirth, *RömMitt* 42 (1927) 45ff.; L. Curtius, *Die Wandmalerei Pompejis* 102ff. Exact dates for the transition from the second to the third Pompeian style are also missing. We can only ascertain a relative development leading from the House of Livia to the Tiber House on the Palatine. Curtius, *ibid.* 123ff. related the garlands of the first one to those of the Ara Pacis. Both are the most perfect examples of ancient representations of garlands, cf. E. Napp, *Bukranion und Girlande*, diss. Heidelberg (1933) 41, and worthy of an epoch which would arrange flowers and fruit like Vergil's Korydon, *Ecl.* II.45ff. We get at least a lead from the garlands for the dating of the Tiber House, *ibid.* 43. Napp dated them 10 A.D., Curtius somewhat later; see also M.I. Rostovtzeff, *Mystic Italy* 113. Some of the Farnesina's inventions seem to be related to earlier Augustan monuments as the archaistic winged women among vines which appear in the *ala sinistra* of the House of Livia and on Campana reliefs, Rohden and Winnefeld (supra n. 16) pl. 62, 1; cf. the fragment *NSc* (1901) 122, fig. 86. Moreover, it turns out that the Augustus portrait of the fragment goes back to an early one of the young Augustus. The process would correspond to the one which led at the same time to the creation of the posthumous portrait of the boy, cf. O. Brendel, *Ikonographie* 30 and J. Sieveking, *RömMitt* 48 (1933) 303. This again is a return to the world of ideas of between 40 and 25 B.C. which includes classical Augustan poetry.

27. Vergil, *Ecl.* I. 42, *Hic illum vidi iuvenem . . .*

28. *Ibid.* 63, *. . . quam nostro illius labatur pectore voltus.* W. Weber, *D. Prophet u. sein Gott* 38, rightly emphasizes that these words refer to the portrait.

29. Suetonius, *Augustus* 95. 8ff. W. Déonna, *La reconnaissance de l'enfant divin*, *RHR* 83 (1921) 192.

30. Horace, *Carmina* IV. 5. 5. *Instar veris enim voltus ubi tuus adfulsit populo gratior it dies . . .*

31. *RömMitt* 26 (1911) 36, with illustration; this, however, refers mainly to the sacred landscape of the background.

32. *MAAR* (supra n. 3) pl. 5, 1.

33. The sacred landscape in Naples, *Mus. Naz.* 12, pl. 8, shows a similar building with a sphinx and a

statue as telamons.

34. Rostovtzeff (supra n. 26) 41, fig. 18, where similar metal vases are shown; for their meaning see 131f.
35. Supra n. 1 pl. 1 and 5.
36. Paribeni, *Mus. Naz.* (1932) 187, no. 478/79. Dionysus alone would not be so unusual because he and his circle are preferred as supporting figures during the Roman Empire, perhaps even earlier; cf. E. Wurz, *Plastische Dekor. des Stützwerkes* 64f. Best known are the supporting satyrs of the Athenian Dionysus theatre, R. Herbig, *D. Dionysostheater in Athen* 10, W. Froehner, *Catal. Louvre* 275 or Copenhagen, Glyptothek 497/98. I wish to thank Curtius for the following reference: satyr and caryatid together as architectural support, Constantinople, Cat. Musée impérial, G. Mendel 1130. Also herms for similar use: temple of Mercury on coins of Antoninus Pius, M. Bernhart, *HAW* pl. 92, 1, four herms as telamons; now in Lateran, Benndorf-Schöne 310, pl. 19; S. Reinach, *RepRel.* 3, 283, urn in Brit. Mus., *Ancient Marbles* 5, pl. 4.
37. *No. 265 and 267*, both according to Visconti from the Villa of the Quintilii; no. 265 incorrectly named Asclepius. The lower part of the modius is correctly restored. For the uncertain place of origin cf. T. Ashby, *Ausonia* 4 (1909) 60. Both pieces are indeed listed as old Giustiniani property in *Galleria G.* II pl. 44. The state of preservation is mediocre. The following are my notes:
    No. 265, Sarapis. Height from slab to beard, 0.755 m. The herm and front of modius are restored, the face is touched up.
    No. 267, Africa. Height from slab to chin, 0.66 m. Restored are the herm, horns, ears and trunk; their existing sockets prove that the three last ones are correct. The nose and chin are modern. The kalathos and slab are ancient and unbroken.
38. For the history of this personification, including the picture in the tondo of the cup from Boscoreale, *MonPiot* 5 (1899) pl. 1, see J. Bayet, *MélRome* 48 (1931) 44ff. Only no. 267 has a modius.
39. Lehmann-Hartleben, examining table legs with mythological figures, arrived at similar observations, *RömMitt* 38/39 (1923-24) 277. See also the Egyptianizing telamons of red granite in the Sala Croce Greca of the Vatican, Helbig, *Führer*[1] 30. Similar telamons serve as identification of the precinct of Isis on the well-known relief in the Mus. Naz., Paribeni (supra n. 35) no. 103.
40. For a survey, *MythLex* 1406f., s.v. "Sphinx."
41. Suetonius, *Div. Aug.* 50. Pliny, *N.H.* 37. 4. Cf. F. Studniczka, *RömMitt* 25 (1910) 30.
42. H. Mattingly, *Coins Rom. Emp.* I pl. 17, 6.
43. Alföldi (supra n. 25) 370 and *RE* 2083f., 2094, s.v. "Sibylle."
44. R. Herbig, *RE* 1749, s.v. "Sphinx."
45. Milani, *StudMat* 2 (1902) 178; cf. Curtius, *RömMitt* 49 (1934) 144; H. Berve, *Der Kaiser Augustus* (1934).
46. Rohden-Winnefeld (supra n. 16) pl. 114, 2; cf. pl. 44.
47. Ippel (supra n. 26), see for survey of Egyptianizing details in the Farnesina. They alone do not indicate an Alexandrian origin of the entire style; among opposing facts is the Seleucus inscription, cf. Curtius (supra n. 26) 126; for architectural landscape, Rostovtzeff (supra n. 26) 135ff. Cf. G.E. Rizzo, *Pittura ellenist.* 2. It is understandable that Egypt aroused interest everywhere at this time; one could even expect the golden age to come from there, W. Tarn, *JRS* (1932) 137ff.
48. Poimandres 176. G. Pasquali, *Orazio lirico* 182. E. Norden also suggested a provenance from the Pharaonic cult, cf. Alföldi (supra n. 25) 379.
49. W. Kroll, *RE* 15, 1, 979f. Also *CIL* 6, 100, no. 519.
50. Hermes Ludovisi, Helbig no. 2326; G. Lippold, *RE* s.v. "Kleomenes." New replica from Anzio, Museo Nazion. Romano, *Gnomon* (1932) 506. Additional preserved parts show that the left hand did not hold the moneybag as was the opinion of Studniczka, text ABr 1001, 12; it was a *kerykeion*. It belongs there, but its position changes according to the copyist; the *kerykeion* held by the so-called Germanicus in the Louvre seems to have been lowered like that of the Mercurius-Augustus discussed here. For the portrait see ch. III.
51. W. Fröhner mistook it for the gesture described by Apuleius, *Met.* 2. 21.1ff.; cf. J.J. Bernoulli, *Röm. Ikonographie* I 229. The gesture is known from representations of debating scholars. Examples: sarcophagus in Palermo, *AJA* 31 (1927) 294, with standing philosopher at the right corner; Zeno on the cup with skeletons from Boscoreale, *MonPiot* 5 (1899) pl. 8, 1. From a gesture which strongly resembles the arrangement of the fingers of the Kleomenes statue, Early Christian art developed the image of Christ as Logos; cf. K. Sittl, *Gebärden* 304.

52. *Acts* 14: 12ff.
53. Cicero, *De nat. deorum* 3. 22. 56; cf. Scott (supra n. 2) 30.
54. For the agreement between poetic and pictorial testimonies of Augustan religion, see M.I. Rostovtzeff, *RömMitt* 38/39 (1923–24) 289.
55. For the development of this concept of Mercury in the emperor cult of the provinces, and its historical situation, see Bickel, *BonnJbb* 133 (1928) 13ff., esp. 17ff. Perhaps we should mention here the strange interpretation which Macrobius gave of the imperial form of the *kerykeion* which is used here, because he believed it to be Egyptian, *Sat.* 1. 19. 7: *In Mercurio solem coli etiam ex caduceo claret, quod Aegyptii in specie draconum maris e feminae coniunctorum figuraverunt Mercurio consecrandum. Hi dracones parte media voluminis sui in vicem nodo, quem vocant Herculis, obligantur,* etc. Cf. Minervini, *BdI* (1842) 159.
56. Thot-Basileus: *MythLex* 853, s.v. "Thot." The Egyptian royal year had throughout history begun on the first day of Thot, cf. B. Pick, *ZfN* 14 (1887) 297. It remains doubtful, however, whether Kerenyi (supra n. 8) 160, was right in assuming a special relationship between Augustus and Thot because 31 August 30 B.C. and Thot 1 coincided; cf. also V. Gardthausen, *Augustus* 2, I, 244f. When at this time the calendar was reformed, 29 August became Thot 1, not 31 August. Incidentally, the original Sextilis has been called August only since 8 B.C., which means much later and for different reasons; cf. *RE* 62, s.v. "Monat." Yet Thot, the month of the emperor's birth, becomes Sebastos; Herzog-Hauser, *RE* suppl. 4, 822.
57. Reitzenstein, *Poimandres* (supra n. 48). The commentary by Kiessling-Heinze (supra n. 24) 17, starts with the same considerations. Cf. Bickel (supra n. 55): "Der ursprüngliche Handelsgott Mercurius des republikanischen Italiens reicht für die Horazische Vorstellung nicht aus." Scott (supra n. 2) 29, 32. An old Roman Mercury as god of peace existed also, F. Altheim, *Röm. Religionsgesch.* 3, 62. This does not exclude other meanings but, on the contrary, facilitates their unification.
58. Horace, *Carmina* II. 17.29. This line also has an astrological meaning which F. Boll, *Philologus* 69 (1910) 164, has interpreted. The meaning of Mercurialis is probably ambiguous, astrological as well as real, cf. Kiessling-Heinte (supra n. 24) 233. For the organization of the priestly colleges, where the mother Maia also held a position, see W. Kroll, *RE* s.v. "Mercuriales." For Mercuriales as mystics, Kerényi (supra n. 8); Scott (supra n. 2) 227ff.
59. Supra n. 31.
60. Cf. E. Norden, *Geburt des Kindes* 57f., 147; W. Weber (supra n. 28) 39f. In Vergil Augustus himself says: *Pascite ut ante boves . . .* The same ideas occur again in Horace, *Carmina* IV. 5: *tutus bos etenim rura perambulat, nutrit rura Ceres almaque Faustitas . . .*
61. For the concept of *Pia gens* and *Pietas saeculi*, Alföldi (supra n. 25) 375. According to Curtius even the victories of the center panel and the female half figure with a blossom, who is between them, could be part of these ideas, *MAAR* (supra n. 3) pls. 1, 2: *Spes Augusta and Victoria Augusti;* see J. Gagé, *RA* 34 (1931) 2, 30ff.
62. Supra n. 50.
63. Bernoulli, *Röm. Ikonographie* I 231, already found the old name Germanicus untenable. For his portrait, see Curtius (supra n. 44) 127. The first to call him Augustus was J.P. Six, *RA* 4 (1916) 257ff. Cf. Studniczka, text *Abr* 1001, 12; Lippold (supra n. 50); Scott (supra n. 2) 24. P. Graindor, *Athènes sous Auguste* 233, added new arguments in favor of this idea.
64. *Ibid.* 259.
65. O. Brendel, *Ikonographie des Kaisers Augustus* 40ff, Type C. For the head, see Curtius, *Antike* 7 (1931) 250f.
66. For the dating of the inscription, see Graindor (supra n. 63) 232.
67. Studniczka (supra n. 63). M. Collignon, *Statues funér.* 316ff.
68. Sala Croce Greca 561.
69. A. Levi, *Sculture* no. 142, pl. 76, 77.
70. Supra n. 63.
71. *ARW* 18 (1915) 23f; O. Weinreich, *Menekrates Zeus* II.
72. *Ibid.* 17.
73. *RE* Suppl. 4, 816, s.v. "Kaiserkult"; for examples see Alföldi (supra n. 25) 376–8, 383.
74. *De Domo* 34, 92. Corresponding ideas are later transferred to Augustus and Octavia; cf. the interpretation of Vergil by O. Immisch, *Aus Roms Zeitenwende* 33.
75. Cf. G. Wissowa, *Röm. Rel.* 305, 3. Kroll, *RE* 980 s.v. "Mercurius." Scott (supra n. 2) 230.
76. I. Scott Ryberg, "Rites of the State Religion in Roman Art," *MAAR* 22 (1955) 39, pl. 10, fig. 20.

77. Supra n. 25, 384.
78. Cf. Graindor (supra n. 63).
79. Catal. Drouot 26, no. 145 with illustration.
80. Cf. the silver cup from Boscoreale, *MonPiot* 5 (1899), pl. 24 with kantharos behind the head of Dionysus, *kerykeion* behind the head of Hermes on Roman lamp, Coll. Loeb, Sieveking, *Bronzen, Terrak.* etc. pl. 28, 1.
81. *Catal. Gems* 434, pl. 84 and 85.
82. Studniczka (supra n. 63). P. Marconi, *BdA* 26 (1932) 157, fig. 12 for the beautiful head in Ancona.

Fig. 1. Le Grand Camée de France, Paris, Bibliothèque Nationale, Cabinet des Médailles

Classical "Ariels"

In THE UPPER PART of that precious stone usually known as the *Grand Camée de France* (Fig. 1) the Emperor Augustus is represented in the center*. His transfigured apparition forms part of a celestial scene which, in spirit, entirely conforms to the fanciful language current at the Roman court about anything regarding the imperial person. In poetry Ovid was a master of this style. Augustus in heaven, flanked by two early-deceased descendants of his house, is witnessing an event that is being celebrated in the theater of earthly reality below, even there curiously interspersed with much allegorical detail. This event shall not further occupy us here.[1] Yet centering upon it his august attention, the late emperor appears above, dressed in a white toga (the fold of which falls solemnly down behind his shoulders), wearing a radiate crown on his head, and clasping a scepter in his right hand. He is represented as calmly reclining on the back of a huge figure in Persian dress as though on a veritable couch,[2] and as being serenely carried through, rather than toward, the aerial spaces. This strange looking carrier, who holds a globe in his hands, has no wings, but seems rather to be quietly floating in an almost horizontal position, the face in profile and slightly raised like that of a swimmer, and the outstretched legs lightly moving, like oars, in the air. It is here that the old question occurs which we wish to take up once more. Who is the Persian?

The question has been often discussed, and illustrations of the scene are easily available.[3] Further description may for the moment be dispensed with. As to the specific problem of the Persian, the last answer given is that he represents Alexander the Great. L. Curtius, to whom this suggestion is due,[4] has the merit of having recently examined and of having, with a vast knowledge of the problems involved, finally established the identity of most of the historical personages represented on the *Grand Camée*. Tiberius and Livia at the center, Augustus above, have long been known as the main characters, but even more significant for an exact understanding of this historical monument is Curtius' identification of the figure with the shield above at the left as the Younger Drusus,[5] an identification which is, I think, incontestable. Drusus died in 23 A.D., and since his image here already occurs among the celestials, the recorded date of his death becomes a hinge on which all remaining denominations must depend, especially those of the younger members of the family still on earth. Indeed, it seems that we have now to consider the representation on the cameo as illustrating the status of the Claudian family between the years 23 and 29 A.D., when the dowager empress Livia also passed away, for on the cameo she is portrayed among the living. In general, the renewed examination of the princely

Fig. 2. Le Grand Camée de France, detail, Paris,
Bibliothèque Nationale, Cabinet des Médailles

Fig. 3. Alexander the Great, silver tetra-
drachm, minted by Lysimachus

portraits has proved highly informative with regard to the political and personal conditions mirrored in the composition, and this result is in keeping with the official and almost documentary character of the monument itself. But the situation seems different with regard to the curious Persian. He definitely is not one of the Claudian group, and, though a stranger, he does not behave like one obliged to be present against his will, as does the mourning Parthian prince, his earthly counterpart, beside the throne of Livia. Granted his likeness to Alexander as the latter is depicted on his coins (Figs, 2, 3),[6] it must be asked whether any likeness of portraits can decide a case like this, if it does not at the same time explain the particular role allotted to the figure in the composition. It seems to me that this consideration does not favor the identification of the figure as Alexander. The task of carrying another person on his back is too conspicuous a part of this character, and is neither in itself suitable to a representation of Alexander, even if the man thus carried is the deified Augustus, nor does any analogy to this representation seem to exist among the well-known portraits of Alexander the Great, so often and so variably reproduced in classical art, or among the portraits of any other antique personality of equal rank and standing. And if the Macedonian hero was, indeed, to be represented in this unusual attitude, the Persian attire, no less uncommon for him, together with the absence of any insignia except the highly ambiguous globe,[7] would make it only the more difficult to recognize him. In spite of the significant results achieved by previous research on the Paris cameo, the point remains doubtful whether a character thus described and thus employed in a work of the Imperial epoch can, in accordance with the ideas then current, be at all understood as a representation of Alexander.

For this reason, I should like in this paper to pursue somewhat further another possible approach to the elusive Persian, thus postponing for a while the question of portrait-likeness entirely. This second line of research, which likewise has previously been indicated by Curtius,[8] has the one advantage of demonstrating, with rich material, that the figure of the Persian, whoever he be, is by no means unique with regard to the function entrusted to him in the composition of the cameo. This function, which at the very least consists in the task of carrying the deified Augustus through the heavens, aligns the carrier with a number of other representations similar in idea and significance, namely the various physical means of ascension.

These form a fairly extended chapter in Roman art, as is well known. The vehicles of ascension, indeed, were manifold. The one which seems most natural, and certainly was one of the oldest and most venerable among them, was the car drawn by horses, which are sometimes winged, but as often are not.[9] This idea has proved particularly persistent. I still recall a certain song, the somewhat monotonous tune of which was heard from children all along the streets of my home town, Nuremberg, when in the early evenings of spring they were playing their modest outdoor games on the sidewalks:

> Ein alter
> Posthalter
> Von siebenzig Jahr'n,
> Der wollt mit

> Sieben Schimmeln
> Zum Himmel
> Einfahrn. . .

I do not remember what happened to the "alter Posthalter" later in the song, but the unexpected way in which the horses of his obsolete profession unexpectedly but convincingly turn to become the tools of his anticipated ascension, probably is impressive enough to stick in anyone's memory, even at an age when the wealth of apparent symbolism in these obscure verses was hardly realized by either singers or hearers. In order to appreciate the astonishing idea of a chariot, and especially of an old mail-coach, drawn heavenward by seven white horses, it is not necessary to remember that, incidentally, seven is also the number of the planets. Nor is there any certainty, or even probability, that the originators of this little piece of "Volkspoesie" were themselves aware how aptly they had equipped their anonymous hero for his celestial enterprise. Seven has from old been a significant number, and the idea of the ascension by car is an ancient formula. Such old formulae of human imagination survive and are easily combined with each other for the sake of their inherent impressiveness, rather than on the ground of adequate understanding.

Yet besides the car, moved by more or less supernatural forces, individual animals served the classical artists equally well for embodying their conceptions of mythical or allegorical ascension. Birds might naturally become the winged carriers of elected souls; thus Homer is seen in the decoration of the well-known silver tumbler at Naples[10] seated between the spacious wings of an enormous eagle, which was supposed to carry the godlike poet toward a goal which, however undefined, certainly lay beyond the limits of earthly life. Perhaps this goal is not even so indefinite as it might seem at first sight. High up at the right, in the direction toward which the eagle is flying, a swan appears with extended wings. It goes without saying that the presence of Apollo's bird very suitably stresses the force and the divine character of that inspiration which leads the poet, as in life, so here, on his lofty way. That is to say, the swan is probably introduced in this scene as an inhabitant of Apollo's fabulous country, the land of the Hyperboreans, an abode, so the ancients thought, of blessed souls. As swans are said to guide distinguished spirits the long way, not otherwise accessible, to the eternally happy Hyperboreans,[11] there is a good chance that the swan represented on the tumbler of Naples is doing the same, and that, in the ways of mythological imagery, the destiny of Homer is there described with considerably greater precision than can at first be recognized. He is being carried away to a life of Hyperborean pleasures suitable to a seer and a singer. The silver tumbler is a work of the early Imperial epoch, though created under a strong Hellenistic influence. Not long before this time, and equally relying on predominantly Hellenistic metaphors, Horace had described himself as becoming a swan, and in this shape eventually reaching, a *canorus ales*, the Hyperborean fields.[12] The apotheosis of Homer, as represented on the little drinking vessel, evidently was based on ideas similar to those of which Horace also had made use. Still, since the country of the Hyperboreans is a place of mythical, more than geographical definition, the eagle might have been found quite as appropriate a bird for carrying the deified poet; for else-where in ancient belief we find eagles entrusted with the task of transferring the deified soul from its earthly to its better life in a world of eternal light, a life in the sun.[13] Two eagles, for example, are depicted on the base of the Column of An-toninus Pius in the Vatican Museum as accompanying the spirits of Antoninus and Faustina on their journey through the skies (Fig. 4).[14]

How far removed these friendly carriers seem from the rapacious monsters—som-bre birds or winged sphinxes with unmoved faces—who in earlier Greek art, even on the throne of Phidias' Great Zeus, had been shown carrying off the vainly resisting mortals![15] But the much later representations which we are here considering should be understood against the background of those older, and much more superstitious, ideas. The concept of human souls carried away by winged beings, and received by air and sky, forms a basic concept common to both ways of thinking. It will soon be seen that this dark background was never quite forgotten, but that at all events the philosophical attitude prevailing during the Roman epoch at least afforded a chance to interpret the century-old images in a more friendly way. This growing freedom of interpretation which was applied to the old and deep-rooted ideas of human after-life in the sky naturally made for a greater variability in the rendering of such ideas even in the arts. Thus, in Roman art, the monsters of old tales were seldom, if ever, used in order to illustrate the rape of souls, which in turn assumed more and more frequently the form of a regular ascension. Nor was any need felt to restrict the means of ascension depicted in art to a species of natural fliers, such as birds are. In a third type of representations the ascension of human beings, particularly of notable persons, is effected not by chariot and horses, nor by birds like the eagle, but by mythical or allegorical figures, often equipped with wings and thus enabled to per-form their ethereal task. In these cases the person or persons carried are regularly represented as reclining on the back of the carrier, just as Augustus is reclining on the back of the mysterious Persian. No doubt, the representation on the Paris cameo belongs to this latter type. But a serious difficulty arises from the fact that in this type of representation, so far as we now know, there are not many examples in which the carriers are rendered alike. If the carrying figures represent personifica-tions, as seems probable from the outset, they must be held to express a different idea in every case. They are deliberately chosen for some individual purpose, and thus require individual explanations wherever they occur. There was, in brief, no single and definite name by which the forces carrying man to immortality could be unequivocally called. If these forces had to be personified, or otherwise to be made visible, it had to be done by making a free use of mythical or symbolical allusions, in order to make the rendering intelligible to all, or intelligible at least to the erudite.

In the relief of the Conservatori Palace, mentioned in note 2, the deified Sabina is represented as being transported on the back of a feminine winged creature which holds a torch (Fig. 5). In the series of coins issued to commemorate the deification of the elder Faustina, the same scene occurs with the added legend *Consecratio*.[16] The chance is, and should not be overlooked, that the legend may refer to the female figure which in this case is carrying the deified Faustina. Scenes of *Consecratio* are

Fig. 4. Apotheosis of Antoninus and Faustina, Rome, Musei Vaticani

Fig. 5. Apotheosis of Sabina, wife of Hadrian, Rome, Palazzo dei Conservatori

not seldom represented in Imperial coinage, mostly in the traditional way of the *ascensio per aquilam*,[17] but also by other familiar means as, for instance, the flying chariot. The commemorative series with the portrait of Faustina further comprises the image of a car drawn by elephants, and other coins show empresses riding on a flying peacock, both of these animals stressing the aspect of eternal life so closely connected with the consecration. The same idea can, moreover, be expressed by seven stars, the seven planets, hovering around the moon. All of these representations, if connected with the proper legend, show by visible signs the act, or the fact, or the result of consecration. But only the one coin, commemorating the deification of the elder Faustina, introduces into these familiar types a human figure as the means by which the consecration is effected. The figure is female, and it is winged, but the torch it carries neither fits the conception of a simple *Victoria*, nor of *Aeternitas*. Why do we not call her *Consecratio*? This name, suggested by the very legend, would make her a good Latin personification. Why consecration personified should hold a torch becomes quite intelligible from the relief of Sabina, where the winged figure must, of course, have the same meaning as on the coin. There the figure aptly carries the flame, pointing skyward, of the pyre out of which consecration arises. However, consecration cannot come about by itself alone, without proper action, taken in this case by the emperor. Therefore Hadrian is shown to be present in an official posture, and with a very strange gesture. I think that the message of the relief in the Conservatori Palace should be read as follows: Hadrian is sending the deified empress to heaven by a formal decree of consecration. *Consecratio*, a most legal and a very Roman procedure, is personified in the shape of a winged woman demonstrated to be the vehicle by the help of which Sabina becomes, to quote another formula familiar to Roman coinage, *sideribus recepta*.

But the "Apotheosis of Sabina" constitutes a comparatively simple case. Unfortunately, the same cannot be said about two other figures which, from their function and partly also from the equipment with which they are portrayed, form the closest parallels known till now to the Persian of the great cameo, and which for this reason have already been compared with the representation on the cameo by Curtius. These are a winged man in Persian attire, depicted on the ceiling of the so-called subterranean basilica in Rome as kidnapping Ganymedes (Fig. 6),[18] and the youthful *Genius*, likewise winged, who carries Antoninus and Faustina in the relief, previously mentioned, of the base in the Vatican (Fig. 4).[19] Both figures, indeed, show great and significant similarities to the Persian in the cameo, and therefore deserve our full attention. But it should be stated at the outset that the points in which they can be compared with the Persian are not the same in each case. The *Genius* of the Antoninus base is comparable to the Persian here under discussion because both figures apparently carry deceased Roman emperors, and because both, in addition to the august burden on their backs, hold a globe in their hands. Both these points do not hold good with the other figure, which forms part of the decoration of the subterranean basilica. This figure is a part of a well-known mythical scene, though rendered in a rather unusual way, and it has no globe. But it does wear the Persian costume, which in turn is found lacking in the *Genius* of the Antoninus base; and ac-

Fig. 6. Rape of Gaymedes, detail of ceiling, Rome, Basilica
Sotterranea

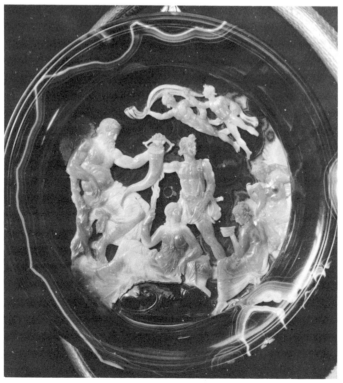

Fig. 7. Tazza Farnese, Naples, Museo Nazionale

tion and wings alike show it to be another aerial being just as are the two others. Who are these two figures?

The *Genius* on the base of the Column of Antoninus is portrayed as a youth with a round face framed by long curls and fully turned toward the spectator, the body stretched out in the position commonly indicating upward flight. He is nude, for the little fluttering cloak behind the back hardly serves any other purpose than to indicate the swiftness of his movement. In his left hand he lightly balances a sphere, surrounded by the zodiacal ribbon, on which the astral signs of ram, bull, and fish are discernible, besides the crescent. A snake seems to creep toward the top of this globe, past the arm of the figure, so that the coiling end of the serpent's tail hangs free in the air.

The figure is not easy of interpretation. The suggestion that it may represent *Aeon*, put forward first by L. Deubner, seconded by others,[20] seems the most satisfactory explanation yet given. But the explanation is not certain. There is no other definitely known instance of the personified abstraction "eternity" to support the application of this name to the *Genius* on the Antoninus base, and the one other male figure in antique art which, according to our present knowledge, may have a legitimate claim to the same title, looks different and has no wings.[21] Thus, the case is still pending, although the solution *Aeon* should be regarded as at least possible. On the other hand, this *Genius* apparently is a male counterpart of the *Consecratio* who carries Sabina. The female designation cannot be applied to him, for obvious reasons, but it may seem worthwhile to follow the indication of iconographical logic contained in this statement, and to ask whether there is in Latin usage another term that conveys the same or a kindred significance, though of masculine gender. It seems, in fact, that such a term exists. The *Genius* of the Vatican base cannot be the personified *Consecratio*, but he can be the personified *Ascensus*. This is, indeed, what I should like to suggest. Not only can this name, or one of similar meaning, satisfy the strictest interpretation we can think of for the winged figure and its function, but it would also explain the reason why the figure is so conspicuously placed in the center of a composition which forms the main side of a base designed to support a column dedicated, as the coins put it, *Divo Pio.*[22] The composition precisely records the ascension by which Antoninus became the *Divus Pius*. Nor did this personification need to be invented particularly for the purpose to which it is here used. *Ascensus* was a god, or a deified function, of old standing in Roman religion, and for that matter had a good and genuinely Roman sound.[23] Also the name and significance of *Ascensus* will very likely facilitate the explanation of the globe which the winged figure holds in its left hand. This is a celestial sphere, as the zodiac shows, and the serpent may therefore here, as in other examples, denote the heavenly path of the sun.[24] If so, it would at the same time indicate the road which the blessed spirits follow, and the eventual goal for which they are bound. In following the serpentine route of the steep ways of the sun they will pass by the realm of the moon, itself an abode of happy souls;[25] finally they will reach the very top of the universe, just where the serpent's head is placed in the relief, and there the ascension will end.

Therefore, if *Ascensus* is its name, the figure is distinctly characterized as an

Ascensus ad Superos and, from the point of view of classical iconography, has become an aerial being to which the name of *Zephyrus* or of any other gentle "Ariel" of antique mythology might as well be given, were it not for the globe and the serpent. Especially in works of late classical art, which made such lavish use of old and new symbols, similar figures were seen quite often, but not even by the contemporaries were they always easily defined. One instance of an apparent difficulty of interpretation, occurring in John of Gaza's description of the now entirely lost representation of the *Kosmos* in the winter baths at Gaza, may be briefly mentioned because it concerns a case apparently relevant here. John mentions a figure of a winged angel, as he calls it, forming part of this painted cosmography; around the neck of the "angel" a snake is wound, and he is holding the earth, which is kept floating in the midst of the air by all the winds.[26] Since the earth in a composition of this kind can hardly have had any form other than that of a globe, somehow supported by the angel, the latter must even in this respect have looked quite similar to the winged *Genius* of the Antoninus base. Of the serpent, likewise present in both representations, but clearly in a different function, John ventures an explanation of his own, while for the figure he offers no name, probably because he found no name inscribed near it in the original which he was describing. Unfortunately, his own description is hardly definite enough to allow a safe reconstruction of the figure. Yet in general trend the passage is best compared with the prayer of Socrates in Aristophanes' *Clouds:* "Oh, Lord and Master, immeasurable Air, who keepest the earth in the midst of space."[27] Evidently the idea is the same as the one which John found expressed in the winged carrier of the earth portrayed at Gaza. It may therefore be concluded that this troublesome angel, or *Genius,* also represented the "Air, supporting the earth," the more so since the related character, *Aither,* was seen, likewise winged, in another section of the Gaza composition. What part the four winds had in the symbolical combination, if they were at all shown, is not so clear. But it is pertinent to remember that there was a general tradition on which to base the visualization of various aerial forces, not of the winds alone; and that equipping the beings representing such powers with a symbolical globe was not something unheard of. The winged *Ascensus* of the Vatican base falls in line with these ideas, although his globe is not the earth, but the universe.

Different from this and the preceding cases is the rape of Ganymedes among the reliefs of the subterranean basilica in Rome, for a generally known myth forms its subject. There can be no doubt about the figure of Ganymedes. Everybody knew the story and image of Zeus's favorite, and in the form in which he is here shown, in the characteristic attitude of pouring, and in the less conventional torch that was placed in his outstretched left hand, the initiated might, moreover, recognize hints of Ganymedes' future astral destiny, when he, transformed into the sign of *Aquarius,* should eventually adorn our nocturnal sky.[28] Rape and ascension are contracted into one scene. The greater difficulty of interpretation arises when one tries to name the robber. All that is known of him, since his face has been destroyed, is that he has wings and wears trousers that form part of a definitely barbarian costume. It is, therefore, impossible to call him Zeus, who either in person or in the familiar disguise of an eagle usually accomplished the rape; but who could never have appeared in this peculiar attire and therefore must here be substituted for by some other character. This statement of fact may seem strange, but it should be remembered that literary tradition, also, was by no means unanimous in identifying the person, divine or mythical, who abducted Ganymedes.[29] It may still be assumed that the character in the present instance shown to be carrying Ganymedes away, whatever his name, did conform to the words, or at least to the meaning, of a mythical version of which, perhaps, we have no longer knowledge. The representation itself further informs us that this uncommon personality is a genuine inhabitant of the air, a demon[30] rather than a *Genius*, and that he is no Roman, but a barbarian in origin, and most likely a northerner. For this is the one conclusion that can immediately be drawn from his dress, whether we call it Persian, Parthian, Scythian, or Thracian.[31] And who, in classical belief, is the great northerner, hurrying through the air, carrying away mortals, but Boreas, the north wind?[32] From all the indications given, Boreas indeed emerges as the most probable identification of this winged demon, holding Ganymedes in his arms. When, in the Cretan version of the myth,[33] the unfortunate boy was buried in a sacred place by Minos, by whose fault he had perished, the latter is said to have excused himself, reporting that a storm had carried away Ganymedes. There, it seems, the tradition still reflects the old idea that winds transport the souls of men.[34] It is quite possible that another version, now lost, may have connected this idea, the abduction through the winds, in a more definite form with the story of Ganymedes. As the scene is rendered in the subterranean basilica, the abductor cannot be Zeus, nor Minos, nor any of the traditional lovers of Ganymedes, but he can be Boreas. Indeed, the only physiognomical details preserved, the wildly fluttering strands of hair above the forehead, fit this explanation. And the substitution of Boreas for Zeus, whether old or recently invented, would be very much in keeping with the general trend of symbolical interpretation of old myths, characteristic of the decorations found in this odd place.[35] Boreas is not only a northerner; he is a Hyperborean,[36] and it is to the blessed land in the north, or even high up in the sky, that he transports the elected souls.[37] Because in this peculiar representation the astral destiny of Ganymedes has been so purposely stressed, ample reason can be found why an equal emphasis should be given to the northern-Hyperborean origin and destination of the wind god who carries him away. The idea of Boreas as a messenger of Hyperborean pleasures was not at all new and could easily be introduced here; the dress of a foreigner from northern countries would be the natural visible means of referring to it. Thus, Boreas is the name which we would suggest in this case.

But to return to the Persian of the *Grand Camée*. If he is related to the personifications or demons of aerial nature with whom he shares the function of transporting another figure through the sky, he still is not identical with any of them. First, the fact that he has no wings visibly distinguishes him from both Boreas and the personified *Ascensus*. Yet hardly anything conclusive can be deduced from this lack, since the figure is evidently flying even though it has no wings; and since, to cite just one other example, the artist of the famous *Tazza Farnese* (Fig. 7) found no difficulty whatever in portraying his flying wind gods equally wingless.[38] On the basis of costume alone, the figure might as well represent Boreas, in spite of its lack of wings, and a meteorological solution of this sort would even seem preferable to a more political one. For no patriotic Roman, as he looked at the *Grand Camée*, would wish to see a real personality of barbarian, let alone Persian, origin so ostentatiously linked with a symbol that, in the art of the epoch, not infrequently carried a connotation of world ascendancy.[39] And in this representation, the ball of the world belongs to the mysterious Persian, not to Augustus. This is another reason why it seems improbable that the figure should at all represent a political character; but the same reasoning also excludes the interpretation as Boreas, who has no claim to the sign of the globe, and of whose tempestuous nature this quietly floating figure in human shape shows not a trace. From all these considerations it follows that the Persian must be a heavenly apparition, another "Ariel," though in unusual disguise; but in order to decipher his name, it will be necessary to state precisely the double nature of his function. Like a supreme ruler, he holds heaven or the world in his hand, and at the same time, like a servant, he carries Augustus on his back. Perhaps we may be able to solve the riddle of this apparently contradictory position. If it is assumed that the figure itself represents the sky, the hieroglyphic sign of which its hands are grasping, many if not all the difficulties of its explanation will vanish. It has only to be remembered that a personification of the appearance and attire here presented cannot signify the ordinary Roman *Caelus*, because it has nothing in common with the familiar Jupiter-like type of the bearded man, emerging from clouds and unfolding the wide mantle of heaven above his head, who is seen on the armor of the Augustus of Primaporta and in numerous other Roman monuments.[40] This is evidently not the form chosen here to express the underlying idea. However related the present figure may be to other representations of celestial function, neither *Caelus* nor *Caelum* can be the precise translation of its meaning into the Latin language. Still, a term or an intelligible conception to which this image corresponds must exist in Latin thinking and consequently in the Latin language. As it appears to me, such a term can indeed be found if one realizes that it is not heaven in general that has here been made the abode of souls and of Augustus in particular, but that *Caelus* has been substituted for by *Polus*, or, more precisely, by the very summit of heaven, *Polus Borealis*. The so-called Persian personifies *Polus*.

The rest is quickly told. The substitution of *Polus* for *Caelum* is a phenomenon well known in language, favored particularly by the poets of the early Empire, who often use both words as practically synonymous, a usage sanctioned by Varro: *Polus Graecum, id significat circum caeli.*[41] But if *Polus* means heaven, it means the two more definite areas as well where the presumed axis of the universe reaches its highest and its lowest point, and of these two points the one, the northern, supposed to be the upper apex of heaven, always attracted the myth-forming imagination. It was believed to be a region of endless light, the place from which Jupiter, "the highest," wielded his scepter,[42] adorned by the astral signs of the two bears which "see everything,"[43] because they never set below the ocean, and to be the starry field of final happiness that only the most perfect of human souls may ever hope to reach. The basic facts regarding these often-varied ideas are sufficiently known, and need no further discussion. However, it should not be forgotten that *Polus Borealis* was also thought of as the source of cold and frost. It is interesting to observe how one of the brief poems of Martial (IV. 3) exemplifies that the two different ways of considering the celestial north, either as a dwelling of happy spirits or as a source of wintry weather, are by no means incompatible with each other, and indeed were throughout all later antiquity equally valid. The poem explains a snowfall during a spectacle in the open air, which the Emperor Domitian attended, as caused by the little imperial prince deceased in 73 A.D., now gaily playing around the constellations of the northern sky, the two bears or, as the poet has it, Helice and the "Hyperborean Bootes."[44]

If considered against the background of these and similar traditions and expectations, the celestial scene, as such immediately recognizable, of the great Paris cameo gains a new acuteness of meaning, and the idea of a *Polus* personified becomes more understandable. That the idea of this personification was quite within the realm of classical art, and that thus far the explanation suggested of the figure in Persian costume on the great cameo would not constitute a case in itself unique, is attested by a literary notice informing us of another representation of *Polus*, this time the southern pole, found in Byzantium, but now no longer extant.[45] We do not know how the figure of the southern pole was conceived or represented, but just because it did represent the southern pole, its appearance must at any rate have differed from that of the "Persian." For the latter, obviously indicating the abode of the deified Augustus, cannot but signify the northern pole, the place of eternal light, the inhabitants of which look down only in order to realize *quanta sub nocte iaceret nostra dies*.[46] Now Arctos is a neighbor of Boreas;[47] therefore the costume of a northerner fits the personification of the northern sky as well as that of the northern wind.[48] The globe in its hand further stresses its celestial nature, *immensi parva figura poli*,[49] and may even emphasize the preferred position ascribed to the summit of heaven in comparison with other and less lofty parts of the sky. Once these two points, dress and globe of the so-called "Persian," have been clarified, the task of the interpreter ends. If a further description of the heavenly scene were desired, it would have to be given in plain Latin rather than in any other language, or at least as an almost continuous chain of relevant quotations from Latin poets of the epoch. Since the figures of this scene are arranged after the manner of a shallow vault, imitating the very form of heaven seen from earth, the deified Augustus is quite properly shown *inter convexa . . . sidera*, as Ovid liked to address him.[50] But because he is at the same time carried on the back of the celestial pole, his position becomes even more definite than that, and silently bestows on him the importance of a *parens celsique dominator poli*.[51] The *parens* in his light toga, recalling the dazzling white garments of those transfigured,[52] indeed forms the center of a heavenly group portrait as well, of which one figure, probably Germanicus, seated on the well-known Pegasus[53] is being led toward him, while Drusus the Younger approaches him from the other side. The latter is grasping so tightly his shield of honor, his distinguishing attribute,[54] that we are almost forced to the conclusion that this is the very object which secured for him his immortality, and drew him heavenward. Just as it is possible for a Latin poet to say that the lion of Nemea and other conquered monsters "gave" to Hercules "heaven and the stars,"[55] so the silver shield "gives" celestial immortality to Drusus. To carry poetic transformation still further, these persons may themselves become the stars of the particular heaven that is here illustrated, and meet together in a constellation, as Statius says the deified Flavians met on the "great horse" of Domitian: *una locum cervix dabit omnibus astris.*[56] In the scene of the Paris cameo, the group of "stars" would meet on the back of the pole. The idea that, even under such exalted circumstances, some sort of physical support is required in order to make the aerial existence plausible, often looms behind such metaphorical language. The Emperor Julian, for example, speaking in a satirical way of his deified predecessors, describes them as dining in the upper air, that is in a reclining position similar to that of Augustus on the cameo: "the lightness of the bodies with which they had been invested and also the revolutions of the moon sustained them."[57]

One historical observation should be made before these peculiar apparitions are dismissed. The idea of the deified ruler, living on the northern pole of heaven, seems to have originated, not in Rome, but in Pharaonic Egypt, since long before the time of the great Paris cameo, Egyptian kings were declared to occupy the celestial pole, or to shine forth, transformed, as the northern stars.[58] This is an interesting fact which makes the assumption likely that the *Polus* of the cameo may embody a concept perhaps not genuinely Roman, but one introduced into Roman thought from elsewhere. In this case, the source from which the idea slipped into Roman usage can hardly have been any other than the court ceremonial of the Ptolemaic kings of Egypt, where the preservation of a relic of old Egyptian thought, like the setting of the deified ruler in the polar region, will cause no surprise. Indeed, the assumption is not unlikely that the motive had been Hellenized before it became Romanized. It has often been stated that the composition of the Paris cameo must depend on some older and more complete model. If the presumptive model was a work of Alexandrian art, or one executed in the Alexandrian tradition, this supposition would help to explain the occurrence in the composition of a motive based on a predominantly Egyptian idea, and even the fact that the personification used in order to illustrate this motive looks like Alexander would then seem more natural. It probably constitutes a mark of origin rather than a real portrait. At any rate, the figure stands for an idea of presumably Alexandrian coinage, incorporated into Latin usage, as was the underlying word *polus*, and in a Latinized sky it denotes the nocturnal regions where, as every Roman knows, the eye looks for the clear and cold signs around the "stella tramontana."

Notes

*This essay, as it was originally published in a Festschrift in honor of F.W. Shipley, began with the following words: "It is the prerogative of scholars to discuss details. And for a volume dedicated to Dean Shipley, what contribution could be more suitable than an old and much discussed *Quaestio Romana?*"

1. For its controversial explanation see especially the paper of L. Curtius and other literature to which

reference is made infra, n. 4.

2. The position of Augustus on the back of his carrier should be compared, for instance, with that of Sabina, carried to heaven, in the relief of the Palazzo dei Conservatori (Fig. 5); see also J. N. C. Toynbee, *The Hadrianic School* pl. 30, 3. In the cameo, the posture of Augustus is not quite so distinct, because the figure with shield overlaps and entirely obscures the position of the emperor's legs. The figure with the shield, indeed, could hardly interfere in such a way if this part of the composition were in perfect order. It is probably not; see *RömMitt* 49 (1934) 155.

3. See infra n. 4.

4. *RömMitt* 49 (1934) 119ff.; the figure of the Persian, 137ff. For later discussions see A. Holm, *Klio* 13 (1938) 269ff.; F. Poulsen, *Probleme* 33ff. Curtius' interpretation is accepted by J. Gagé, *REA* 37 (1935) 165ff. The various problems of Claudian iconography fall beyond the scope of this paper. Holm, while assenting, together with other recent critics, to the explanation of the Persian as Alexander (*Klio* 13 [1938] 276ff.), doubts whether Augustus is really seated on the back of this figure. But see supra n. 2. Previous explanations, none of them acceptable, of the Persian as Aeneas, Anchises or Iulus, or the Parthian King Phraatakes, sufficiently discussed by Curtius, *op. cit.*, do not require mentioning here.

5. *RömMitt, op. cit.* 124ff. The coins and marble portraits of this prince present factual evidence; assertions to the contrary, like those made by Holm (*Klio* 13 [1938] 274), however forceful, do not prove the contrary.

6. *Ibid.*, 138. For a recent treatment of the coins with portrait of Alexander see Gebauer, *AM* 63–64 (1938–39) 2ff.

7. For both points see also Curtius, *op. cit.* 143ff.

8. *Ibid.* 138ff.

9. For the chariot of fire in the ascension of Elijah, 2 Kings 2:11, and the car as a vehicle of ascension in Roman religious thinking, see E. Strong, *Apotheosis and After-Life* 226ff. Concerning the apotheosis of Herakles by chariot see the extensive previous literature listed by G. M. A. Richter, *AJA* 40 (1941) 370, 13.

10. Illustrated in V. Spinazzola, *Le arti decorative in Pompei* 231. See also K. Lehmann-Hartleben in the article cited infra n. 17.

11. *RE,* XVII, 275, s.v. "Hyperboraeer."

12. Horace, *Od.* II.20; see supra n. 11.

13. F. Cumont, *RA* 13 (1939) 40; idem, *After-Life in Roman Paganism* 158ff. For the emperor on an eagle see Toynbee, *Hadrianic School* pl. 19,1, and infra n. 17.

14. W. Amelung, *Vatikan-Katalog* I, pls. 116–118; W. Helbig and W. Amelung, *Führer durch Rom*[1], 74, n. 123, with previous literature. See also Toynbee, *Hadrianic School* 138, and pl. 30.

15. For birds and sphinxes carrying off human figures see L. Malten, *JdI* 29 (1914) 239ff. Groups of sphinxes assailing youths probably decorated the throne of the Olympian Zeus; for fragments and reconstruction see F. Eichler, *ÖJh* 30 (1936–37) 75ff.

16. For the previous literature regarding the interpretation of the relief showing the ascension of Sabina, see Helbig-Amelung, *op. cit.* 568, no. 990. The coins commemorating Faustina I were recently treated by H. Mattingly, *Coins of the Roman Empire* IV, lviii ff. See infra n. 17.

17. The types of coins to which reference is made in the following are well known and cannot here be discussed in detail. In general see M. Bernhart, *Handbuch zur Münzkunde* II pls. 52–54. Examples of the emperor or empress on the eagle are abundant on coins and other monuments, see K. Lehmann-Hartleben, *Bull. Com.* 62 (1934) 115ff. Faustina I and Faustina II on the celestial chariot, see Bernhart, *op. cit.* pl. 54, 11–12. Empress on peacock, *ibid.* pl. 52, 5; legend "Aeternitas." Group of seven stars with moon, *ibid.* pl. 54, 10. Faustina on back of winged figure with torch, *ibid.* pl. 52, 7. The winged figure is tentatively called Victory, see Mattingly, *op. cit.* 230, or "Aeternitas," see L. Deubner, *RömMitt* 27 (1912) 13; see also Amelung in Helbig-Amelung, *op. cit.* 568, concerning the corresponding figure in the relief of Sabina. Lehmann-Hartleben (*op. cit.* 116) suggested the name of Eos, who might be winged, but who would hardly appear without her traditional pitcher. For the types of "Aeternitas" represented without wings and with different attributes, see Bernhart, *op. cit.* pl. 58, 7–11, and Mattingly, *op. cit.* lxi ff. "Aeternitas" with torch is not certain, *ibid.* lxxxiii.

18. Curtius, *RömMitt* 49 (1939) 139ff.

19. *Ibid.* 138ff.

20. *RömMitt* 27 (1912) 17ff. See supra n. 14, and Curtius, *loc. cit.*

21. For youthful god surrounded by zodiac, on the silver platter of Parabiago, see A. Levi, *La patera*

d'argento di Parabiago, opere d'arte VI. See *AA* (1935) 523. For "Aeternitas," female, see supra n. 17.

22. Bernhart, *op. cit.* pl. 55, 2.
23. Originally, "Ascensus," epithet of an indigenous god, was certainly a prevailingly terrestrial designation; see Tertullianus, *De Nat.* II.15.
24. F. Cumont, *Textes et Monuments . . . de Mithras* I 79; see *AA* (1933) 728.
25. Cumont, *After-Life in Roman Paganism* 96ff; see p. 153 regarding the milky way as path of the sun and the road of the deceased souls to heaven; also A. B. Cook, *Zeus* II 477.
26. John of Gaza, *Ekphrasis* II.45ff. See P. Friedländer, *Johannes v. Gaza* 195ff. For the question whether the building in which John saw the cosmic picture really was in Gaza, his home town, or perhaps in Antioch, and for recent literature, see G. Downey, *Antioch on the Orontes* II (ed. Stilwell) 205ff.
27. V.264. See Ovid, *Fasti* VI.269ff.: *Aere subjecto tam grave pendet onus.*
28. See Cumont, *RA* 8 (1918) 56, and Curtius, *RömMitt, op. cit.* 140. See the previous explanations discussed by Curtius, *loc. cit.*, and not further mentioned here.
29. *RE* VII, 738, s.v. "Ganymedes."
30. Curtius (*op. cit.* 140) calls it a demon of immortality.
31. The custom of wearing trousers was not specifically Persian, but extended to the natives of most regions north of the Black Sea and the Balkans. See *RE* I, 2100, s.v. "Anaxyrides."
32. For Boreas, a Thracian, see Ovid, *Heriod.* XV.343ff.; a Scythian, see Lucan, *Pharsal.* V.603. For Boreas, the robber of souls, see *RE*, s.v., and infra n. 34. In the reliefs of the so-called tower of the winds, in Athens, Boreas is depicted, not in the trouser-costume, but in a heavy dress indicating cold weather, and is clearly distinguished from the milder winds of spring and the hot winds of summer. See *DarSag*, s.v. "Venti." In the calendar-frieze of Hagios Eleutherios (L. Deubner, *Attische Feste* pls. 34ff.), the figure representing winter is heavily dressed, though in a way pointing to a different tradition; see J. C. Webster, *The Labors of the Months* 11, and D. Levi, *Art. Bull.* 23 (1941) 276ff. For a Scythian ploughing the field in autumn, see Deubner, *op. cit.* pl. 36, 8. In the Roman sarcophagi personifying the four seasons as youthful "Genii," the Attis-costume given to winter introduces an identical allusion by way of the northern dress. See the sarcophagus Barberini in Strong, *Apotheosis* pl. 32.
33. See supra n. 29, and the notice of Dosiades in *Schol. Ilias* XX.234.
34. For reference to the winds, carrying away souls, see Cumont, *RA* 13 (1939) 51ff. The youthful gods, robbers of souls, in Thracian or Scythian dress, to whom Curtius previously pointed, *loc. cit.*, probably represent related ideas, but hardly Boreas himself. See *AA* (1938) 356. A "Genius" wearing an apparently Phrygian cap, whose winged head sometimes occurs on clay-arulae from southern Italy, may have some connection with these representational types. His name is not known, but his occurrence proves that similar conceptions had an old foothold in Italy, or at least were familiar to Italian artists. See, for the type in question, I. Scott Ryberg, *An Archaeological Record of Rome* 172, and P. Jacobsthal, *Ornamente* pl. 149b.
35. See J. Carcopino, *La Basilique Pythagorienne* 292ff.; M. I. Rostovtzeff, *Mystic Italy* 138ff.
36. Servius, on *Aen.* X.350: *Boreas de gente suprema . . . In Hyperboreis montibus natus, unde est origo venti Boreae.*
37. *RE*, XVII, 275e, s.v. "Hyperboraeer"; for Hyperboraeans identified with nations of the unexplored north, with Scythians, etc., see *ibid.* 276.
38. A. Furtwängler, *Antike Gemmen* pl. 55; also in Toynbee, *Hadrianic School* pl. 22, 1.
39. See Curtius, *op. cit.* 143ff.; *RömMitt* 51 (1936) 56, n. 1.
40. For references see the literature on the Augustus of Primaporta, a selection of which was recently listed by V. Müller, *AJP* 62 (1941) 496, 1. See also A. Alföldi, *RömMitt* 52 (1937) 55.
41. Varro, *De L. L.* 7, 14.
42. Cumont, *After-Life* 108; the author in *Die Antike* 12 (1936) 285.
43. Ovid, *Trist.* IV. 3.3.
44. For this episode see F. Sauter, *D. römische Kaiserkult bei Martial und Statius* 146.
45. E. Maass, *Tagesgötter* 125.
46. Lucan, *Pharsal.* IX.3, referring to the deified Pompeius.
47. Ovid, *Met.* II.132.
48. The possibility should at least be mentioned that an interesting parallel to the representation of 'Polus" as a northerner might be found on the bronze plaque in Berlin, *AZ* (1854) pl. 65, 3, recently

discussed in A. B. Cook, *Zeus* II 664, and *Ephemeris Archaiol.* (1937) 153. A god in barbarian dress, swinging an axe (Zeus?) and on horseback, is represented together with a veiled figure, two "Kabeiroi" (?), and various cult objects. This group is supported by a human figure, stretched out horizontally, obviously flying in the air. Below are astral signs—ram, bull, and fish, just as on the globe held by "Ascensus" in the Antoninus base—beside *krater* and *corvus*. Unfortunately, this unusual monument cannot be discussed sufficiently on the basis of the drawing published, as long as no photographs are available. The drawing cannot be reliable on all points. It seems that the flying figure wears a Persian or Phrygian hood, but this is not certain. However, the function of the figure is so similar to that of the "Persian" on the great cameo that the former should at least be examined as another possible example of the personified "Polus." If this explanation holds good, the god in the center of the bronze plaque would be characterized as dwelling on the heights of heaven. Is the veiled man (rather than woman) a "soul" received in the upper region of some barbarian heaven? It may be recalled that the pole is a fitting place not only for the Latin Jupiter but for other sky-gods as well; note the Phoenician denomination of Hadad as Baal Saphon, "Lord of the north," Bickermann, *Warburg Journal* 1 (1937) 192.

49. Ovid, *Fasti* VI.278. The pole is "signifer" and (Vergil, *Aen.* I.608) a "shepherd of the Stars"; see Maass, *loc. cit.* These functions can well be illustrated by the sphere placed in the hands of the figure which, thus, is literally made a "signifer."

50. *Ex Ponto* IV.11.129ff.

51. Prayer of Kleanthes to Zeus in Seneca, *Ep.* 107.10.

52. Cumont, *After-Life* 205.

53. For Pegasus or winged horses as vehicles of ascension see Cumont, *op. cit.* 155ff.

54. Curtius, *op. cit.* 124. The shield is represented in perspective foreshortening, and is round rather than oval; see Balsdon, *JRS* 26 (1936) 159, and Holm, *Klio* 13 (1938) 274, on the significance of this question.

55. Martialis, *Epigr.* V.65: *Astra polumque dedit, quamvis obstante noverca, Alcidae Nemees Terror,* etc. See Sauter, *D. röm. Kaiserkult* 147ff.

56. *Silv.* I.1.98; see Sauter, *op. cit.* 149.

57. Julian, *Caes.* 307c; see Cumont, *After-Life* 98.

58. C. Breasted (*Development of Religion* 109ff.) describes the ascent of the Egyptian King to the sky, according to the Pyramid texts: the king flies to heaven "like a falcon," or "the clouds of the sky have taken him away, they exalt king Unis to Re," and so on. On the heights of heaven, "King Neferkere is rowed by the Unwearied Stars, he commands the Imperishable Stars" (p. 139). Or the Pharaoh may be welcomed by Osiris as "lord of the sky" in the place of Re, and join "the Imperishable Stars, the followers of Osiris" (p. 149). The "Imperishable Stars" are in the north of the sky, and are in all likelihood identical with the circumpolar stars, which never set nor disappear (p. 101).

The Shield of Achilles

THE FOLLOWING LITTLE CHAIN of observations and questions relates directly, and more closely than is usually to be expected of works of art, to history and particularly to the special area of political symbolism. There is no other area in which the tension between reality and fancy has repeatedly created such curious relationships. It is a tension which in other areas seems to create an almost unbridgeable gap between art and life. Whoever enters the realm of political symbolism must accustom himself to finding the seemingly clear monuments of historical names and deeds draped, as it were, with the magnificent garments of their secret hopes, their mythical claims and justification. Perhaps the strangest self-pronouncements in history arise where the boundary between appearance and inner meaning becomes a razor-thin line which is easily crossed. These self-pronouncements ceaselessly strive, if not to overcome, at least to direct the mutability in every human situation into the permanence of the spiritual and religious existence of images and symbols. Such attempts are political acts even where they are about to dissolve into the fabulous right before our eyes; this means that they are conditioned by history at the same time as they shape history anew.

We know that the Emperor Caracalla was an outspoken admirer of Alexander the Great. He believed himself to be a successor to this hero in whom the myth of the world-ruler was first truly realized. His strange prepossession was deliberately emphasized to lend a strong justification to his own position and probably accounts for the fortunate circumstance of the finding at Abukir of the famous gold medallion with the portrait of Alexander in armor together with some representations of Caracalla. The medallion is now in East Berlin (Fig. 1). This wonderful work which has gained much renown since its discovery has always been met with surprise and even distrust. To this day we cannot say that all the riddles about its place in the history of art have really been solved. It is immediately evident that it is a mythical portrait in a much wider sense than is common in Greek and Hellenistic art. Thus it has been felt to be amazing and profoundly significant, devised, as it was, precisely at the time when Rome, on the threshold of late antiquity, was becoming increasingly centralized. The face with wide-opened eyes and a Zeus-like forehead reveals a great and tempestuous, indeed a Greek, character, and the slight thrust of the neck towards the right is typical of Alexander's portraits. The small image is adorned and surrounded by weapons serving no other ostensible function than to exhibit significant symbols, just as if the physical characteristics, although they dominate the entire person, are not sufficient for an exhaustive description of the person. For its

Fig. 1. Gold medallion from Abukir, Egypt, Berlin (East), Münzkabinett

Fig. 2. Bronze disk with Caracalla as sungod, Berlin
(West), Antikenmuseum, Staatliche Museen
Preussischer Kulturbesitz

Fig. 3. Cuirass statue from Cerveteri, Rome,
Museo Laterano

Fig. 4. Sun-god, detail of cuirass, statue from Cerveteri,
Rome, Museo Laterano

Fig. 5. Roman statue with cuirass, detail, Turin,
Museo di Antichità

Fig. 6. Portrait of Nero, Worcester Art Museum

Fig. 7. Drawing, the sun-god, Cod. Dc 183, fol. 31r
(9th–10th cent.), Dresden, Landesbibliothek

Fig. 8. Miniature, Emperor Otto II, Cod.
Vat.Lat. 4939, fol. 126r, Rome,
Biblioteca Vaticana

complete interpretation the portrait seems to need the addition of insignia and symbols: thus lance and diadem, thus the exactly rendered armor and shield. They were what intrigued the later Romans about Alexander, since they were the symbols which demonstrated the myth of the world-ruler. Time and again these symbols generated almost incomprehensible forces which affected the entire political history of Hellenism and of the Roman emperors.

This is primarily true of the large, round shield only a third of which is visible on the medallion. Its crowning ornament is nothing other than what is highest in the universe, the starry sky with five of the twelve signs of the zodiac: Aries, Taurus, Gemini, Cancer, and Leo. In the course of the year the sun stays in each of them about one month. Included with them are two heads; one is Sol surrounded by rays, and the other, opposite him, is Luna. Between them are two stars. Towards the center is a female figure, perhaps Nyx, wearing the arched, floating cloak of celestial beings. She appears to be both goddess of the night and ruler of the constellations. The whole representation is of course an abbreviation, necessitated by limited space, but its meaning is clear. The shield itself is actually a picture of the entire firmament, almost a mythological chart of the stars. Because of that it became known to late antiquity as the outstanding weapon in the armory of the world-ruler. It was indeed the grandest symbol of his majesty, since its presence alone was adequate to transform an image of the emperor of the world into one of the emperor of the universe. The claim and title thus revealed, that of "cosmocrator," was well known to those times.

We owe to F. Cumont the discovery that the title "cosmocrator" was a technical term in astrology before it was used to signify the emperor as head of the Roman empire.[1] Cumont's discovery captures the essence of these symbolistic tendencies. Speculations never ceased about the place which should be assigned to the office of emperor, not only among human beings but in the entire animate and inanimate world scheme. While the world of human beings was regarded to an ever greater extent as a duplicate of the cosmos, the universe became a cleverly arranged hierarchy of energies, stars, and elements. Consequently the emperor was seen as analogous to the Prime Mover. We can trace almost literally the same idea in a seemingly different place. Just as the sun moved into a primary position during the progressive organization of the cosmos, so did the emperor, by dint of his title "cosmocrator." He himself became the sun, or, in so far as he was a god, the god Helios. We again find the Emperor Caracalla in armor in the portrait on the bronze disk in West Berlin (Fig. 2). The rays of the sun-god which encircle his head are added for that reason. Even Constantine the Great had a statue of himself as Helios erected in Constantinople.[2] These emperors are all sun-gods by virtue of their office of cosmocrator. It is indeed remarkable how in these ideas the political, religious, and physical concepts of the cosmic image constantly penetrate and shape one another. Cicero had already applied decidedly political terms to the sun, calling it "the leader, prince and ruler of all the other stars."[3] The pictorial tradition followed a similar course. The relief ornament on the armor of a statue from Cerveteri in the Lateran Museum (Figs. 3, 4) offers additional noteworthy evidence. There, on the breastplate of the armor, the sun-god is depicted rising on his quadriga from the sea; underneath are waves delineated in the so-called running-dog pattern. He rises out of the waters, but what kind of sun-god is he? Similar monuments, like the statue in Turin (Fig. 5), a repetition of the Cerveteri one, serve well as controls. We easily recognize the quadriga in its peculiar frontal view. Sol as the sun-god with long hair, dressed in the long tunic of the charioteer, stands in an almost classical pose. In accordance with its placement on the breastplate, the figure stares straight ahead. Occasionally he was taken for a female, Eos, because the charioteer's dress was misinterpreted. But that would scarcely occur to anyone who looked at the statue in the Lateran. Obviously the same device of the sun's rays was used in this image, but several features were changed. Above all the face is different, being unmistakably rounded, with a plump and rather ordinary chin, and framed by short curls instead of streaming, long hair. It is as though one were looking at a smiling tenor ready to sing his part; the divine face, set in a wreath of sunrays, has been replaced by a human one. When, as here, a human being is represented as the sun-god, the transformation makes sense only when it concerns an emperor. For this reason a short mantle, fastened on the right shoulder, a cape such as officers wear, was added to his costume. On the right, the long sleeve, which is part of the charioteer's dress, is visible. Consequently we must seek to identify this sun-god from among portraits of Roman emperors. We might compare portraits of Nero (Fig. 6) and Titus with our round-faced type. A famous colossal statue of Nero was exhibited in Rome at this time and, at least in its later condition, it had the sun-god's diadem of rays.[4] Commodus later replaced Nero's portrait with his own. Cassius Dio commented that: "Some maintain that Nero is represented, others think it is Titus." So, since the close similarity of both portraits caused doubt even in ancient times, we ourselves must leave it at that for the time being. In any case, it is an emperor who stands as cosmocrator in the chariot of the sun. We can see how the myth of the world-ruler has begun to assume the special dogmatic form which was to be its last manifestation in antiquity. Perhaps the Vergilian prophecy from the time of the early principate was still even then remembered. It had predicted that the new world order, the golden age, would be governed by the sun itself: *Tuus iam regnat Apollo* (Thine own Apollo now is ruler), Vergil, *Ecl.* IV. 10. It is most important that these images could absorb so many and such diverse ideas. Though the concept of the cosmocrator had apparently shifted from the sun to the ruler of the universe, the association in turn later on also exerted a decisive influence upon the image of the sun-god (Figs. 7, 8). The old frontal invention with the horses appearing to race in opposite directions resembles a heraldic figure. It especially suited the intentions of late antiquity, which actually absorbed the idea, and it was from there that medieval manuscripts inherited this rather solemn picture of the sun-god.[5] Now Apollo himself stands in his chariot as ruler, crowned with the rays of the sun, his purple cloak flying. Without guiding the chariot he holds the globe in his hand just as the emperor holds the orb. Apollo has again become a world-ruler, and he is shown in the form of his worldly majesty. If the chariot were drawn by eagles and griffins instead of horses, a medieval mythologist would have recognized in the same picture the legendary apotheosis of Alexander the Great.[6]

So strong then is the inner logic of the idea which also manifests itself throughout the pictorial tradition that we ultimately reach its starting point again with the name of Alexander. It is like following a closed circle which thoroughly encompasses the idea of cosmocracy. Its highest subject would be the sun-god, its object the entire world of the stars as the shield of Alexander deliberately reveals it. If one looks at every historical phenomenon for the face of Janus inherent in it, the glance into the future which from late antiquity already perceives the Middle Ages will not suffice; a glance backwards into the past, which only seems to be closed to us, will recover meanings which as a whole are still effective.

The Berlin medallion may well date from the third century A.D., but it could not have been invented that late. The artist must have known an older Alexander portrait, possibly a contemporary one which is unknown to us today. Considering the working methods of copyists, we must ask whether the celestial shield could already have belonged to the original work and whether we can trace its previous older history at all. Perhaps it was merely an addition, derived from the ideas surrounding the concept of the Roman emperor. We know that the comparison of the ruler with the sun was a Hellenistic idea. There remains, however, the strange question of how closely the mythological image of Alexander was related to the historical personality, and how much of it can be ascribed to his ideas about himself. One would have to ask here if the celestial shield, the insignia of the world-ruler, is a motif in the genuine Alexander story, and what role, if any, Alexander himself played with regard to it. We know but little about the weapons of Alexander the Great. With armor, sword, and long spear he presented himself as the military king of Macedonia, which he originally was. Only on a few occasions do we hear about luxurious presents that he accepted. However, there is a rather curious story, obviously a report of a very personal and programmatic action so typical of later Roman emperors, which tells of Alexander's visit to Ilion. At the time of the Persian expedition Alexander considered himself the fulfiller of very old, and, as a matter of fact, Greek ideas. He came from Europe to Asia as an avenger, and at the same time as heir and successor of Achilles, back to whom he proudly traced his mother's family. We read with amazement that a decisive enterprise in Greek history was linked to Homer's poem as if it were its logical consequence. Thus Alexander travels to the tomb of Achilles, he orders games to be performed in his memory, and finally he visits the little sanctuary of the Ilia Athena which was so important to him. There Alexander consecrated his weapons and received others in exchange, which he was told had been kept there since the time of the Trojan war. According to J.G. Droysen, "he made certain to take the sacred shield which allegedly had belonged to Achilles."[7] We have hardly any evidence for this; nevertheless it is certain and it can be easily demonstrated that at that time the shield of Achilles was imagined to have been exactly the same as Alexander's on the medallion of Abukir, that it was a picture of the firmament, a celestial shield.

The well-known Pompeian paintings, for instance, where Hephaistus, the sooty blacksmith, presents his just finished shield to the half-surprised, half-frightened Thetis, again shows a picture of the firmament (Fig. 9). We are tempted for various reasons to contemplate a while longer this well-preserved counterpart to all the later reconstructions of Homer. The beauty of this pictorial invention alone, with the shield as its center, would merit such attention. Our task here, however, is not to describe all the fascinating details of the visit paid by the silver-footed Thetis to the gloomy forge. She went there in order to inspect the weapons that she had sorrowfully ordered for her son. L. Curtius has proved convincingly that behind these pictures is an altered but nevertheless identifiable prototype.[8] Therefore we know exactly how the shield of Achilles must have appeared at that time: it was like the one which its divine maker exhibits for Thetis. He set it up on the anvil in such a way as to make the light flash like lightning off the metallic work of art. It is interesting that of the famous description in the *Iliad* only that part was used which concerns the celestial picture, indicating that it had already completely replaced the old representation of the universe. Although rather cursorily painted, the main constellations of the zodiac are easy to recognize. The large snake which winds its way down through the middle of the shield seems at first puzzling but it can be shown that it is an important sign. Its nearest analogy is the snake on the schematic representation of the world on the so-called Bianchini plaque in the Louvre (Fig. 10), where it occupies the most central of the concentric circles and can therefore be easily identified as the dragon, the long-winding constellation of the celestial pole, which is flanked on the right and left by the two Bears. Accordingly the celestial zones and the pole are clearly indicated with stars between them; the rest is somewhat less clear, least of all the four heads which probably represent the four winds. They actually belong outside the zodiac in the corners of the world and should be grouped like the four celestial women in the old Egyptian world scheme (Fig. 11). From them the way might lead one day to similar images of the Homeric epoch. The Bianchini plaque had also intended a representation of the universe composed in a scientific as well as a poetic manner, according to the knowledge available at that time; later Dante was to do the same. Here in the Pompeian painting, all this is represented in a significantly new way, though it is still reminiscent of Homer who was never forgotten. Though this scene is taken from Homer, it is understood in a different way than the ancients formerly understood their poet. The little winged female behind Thetis is a later addition not mentioned at all in the *Iliad*, but she is in any case a significant addition. As she explains the shield to Thetis, she practices a new discipline that one could call "Homer Studies." Much has to be explained here; the shield's image of the heavens has obviously become an object requiring much thought not only as a work of art, but also specifically with regard to its content. In this respect another version of the same painting which has replaced the winged teacher by a modest maid, or perhaps a Nereid, is important (Fig. 12). This change was possible because the shield no longer exhibits a picture of the firmament, but now rather mysteriously mirrors the likeness of the goddess. Turning to another picture of the firmament (Fig. 13), the winged figure, looking like the wise Muse Urania, reappears with a pointer used by teachers. What does she read and explain? Certainly not the concept of the world-ruler, since it belongs to Alexander and not to the legend of Achilles. What then can the celestial image have conveyed to the goddess to make her seem so startled, so bewildered and

Fig. 9. Thetis and Hephaistus, wall painting from Pompeii, Naples, Museo Nazionale

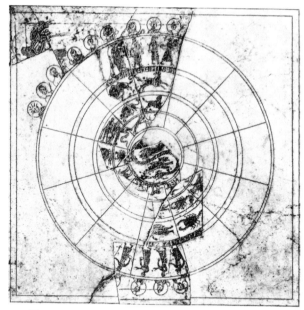

Fig. 10. Bianchini plaque, Paris, Louvre

Fig. 11. Dendera zodiac, Paris, Louvre

Fig. 12. Thetis and Hephaistus, wall painting from Pompeii, Naples, Museo Nazionale

Fig. 13. Thetis and Hephaistus, wall painting from Pompeii, Naples, Museo Nazionale

amazed? It was the fate of her son, which had often been prophesied—Achilles' fate which was seen in the stars, since by that time dead heroes were believed to be carried off to the infinite spaces of heaven rather than to the Elysian fields.[9] Consequently, it is understandable why the pole of the spheres figures so prominently on Achilles' shield: together with the constellations of the Bears it had become the center of the sky and indeed the zenith of the world, the origin of all its movement, the place of eternity, and the abode of its immortals. In all this the image of the hero is consummated and glorified by an epoch which came to see the superhuman and the world above men differently than it had before. Furthermore, the mythical meaning of the celestial shield is linked here with its future interpretation. From the pole of the spheres divine powers move the world; they control it. Suetonius relates how the seven stars of the Little Bear, which appeared as spots impressed on the belly and breast of the new-born Augustus, were the seals of his future empire.

Thus the meanings gradually come together in the image, accumulating as in a treasury. That Imperial Rome was still aware of the fact that the celestial shield had belonged to Achilles before it passed to Alexander is clear from a contemporary coin which shows Hephaistus sitting before his work, which is again the shield with the zodiac (Fig. 14). This image still contains both meanings, one of which is but a revision of the other. This revision, however, was in itself a decisive occurrence in world history: it demonstrates the transition from ancient Greek hero worship to the myth of the cosmocrator and finally to political symbolism. The new myth started with Alexander and was called into existence by his image, but it retained fundamentally the memory of the Achilles story in spite of its difference in character. Vergil's prophecy might still reflect this knowledge, at least in one passage, and that passage is now unexpectedly illuminated from our vantage point. During the years around Caesar's death, when the successor for the orphaned throne of the World Emperor was awaited, while the urgency and the secrecy increased, an old oracle was circulated in Rome which must have been concerned with the impending Parthian war. Vergil included the oracle in his Fourth Eclogue.[10] There the Greek spirit that guided Alexander when he started on his expeditions comes once more to the fore. This will be the last war before the arrival of the golden age. Once more Tiphys will return, once again the swift Argo will sail, *atque iterum ad Troiam magnus mittetur Achilles* (and once again great Achilles will be sent to Troy). Perhaps this element of the Achilles story was not fully incorporated in the concept of the World Emperor because it contradicted the Roman descendancy from Aeneas. They were Trojans, not sons of Achilles. But as G. Rodenwaldt has shown, late antiquity still called the portrait of the emperor in armor, his heroic picture, Achilleic, just as Alexander with his spear was presented as a new hero, a new Achilles.[11] A bronze medallion shows the emperor Florianus (Fig. 15), who ruled only three months, performing an allegorical act. Nothing could demonstrate more sharply the direct contradiction between the transience of a historical figure and the claim of the eternity of his office. The ideas of *restitutio* and *renovatio*—restoration and renovation—already prevail in the Empire just as in the legend on the medallion. They were to become the basis of the medieval title of emperor. For this reason, the emperor stands here in his ar-

Fig. 14. Roman coins with Hephaistus and the shield of Achilles

Fig. 15. Bronze medallion of Emperor Florianus

mor, with a shield beside him as *restitutor saeculi*, the renovator of his shattered epoch. The barely recognizable scorpion on the edge of the shield attests to its uniqueness. The scorpion is a well-known constellation of the zodiac; the shield is a celestial one. By now it is nothing more than an insignia of the office, of the world-embracing title of emperor. Its heroic origin lies far off. But its symbolism, as the more profound memory of the ages, is still remembered.

Notes

1. Cosmocrator and sun-god: F. Cumont, *CRAI* (1919) 322ff., idem, *Die orientalischen Religionen im römischen Heidentum* (Stuttgart, 1959) 276, n. 109; E. Strong, *JRS* 6 (1916) 34f. H. P. L'Orange, *Symbolae Osloenses* 14 (1935) 86ff., and esp. 102ff.

2. Emperor Constantine: T. Preger, "Konstantinos Helios," *Hermes* 36 (1901) 462ff.

3. Cicero on the sun: *Somnium Scipionis* 4, Sol, *Dux et princeps et moderator luminum reliquorum, mens mundi et temperatio.*

4. Emperor Nero represented as "New Sun" on the canvas roof of the Circus Maximus, *Cassius Dio* 63.6.2, cf. F. Sauter, *Der römische Kaiserkult* 142; sources for the Colossus of Nero near the Colosseum, named for him to this day, collected by H. Jordan and C. Hülsen, *Topographie der Stadt Rom* (Berlin, 1871) I 3, 321f. The Colossus wore the rays of the sun-god at least since Vespasian. Nero assumed a wreath of rays also on coins, see H. Mattingly, *Coins of Roman Empire in the British Museum* (London, 1923) I 326ff., pl. 43ff. For source material see O. Weinreich, *Senecas Apocolocyntosis* 44f.; G. Schumann, *Hellenist. und griech. Elemente in der Regierung Neros* diss. (Leipzig, 1930) 24; A. Alföldi, *RömMitt* 49 (1934) 60; and 50 (1935) 107. For Demetrios Poliorketes as sun, see O. Weinreich, *NJbb* 2 (1926) 633ff.

5. Otto II on the triumphal chariot: L. Olschki, "Il ritratto di Ottone nel cod. Vat.lat.4939," *Bibliofilia* 36 (1934) 3ff.

6. Alexander's Ascension: A. Hübner, "Alexander d. Gr. in der deutschen Dichtung," *Die Antike* 9 (1933) 46ff.

7. J. G. Droysen, *Geschichte Alexanders des Grossen*, ed. A. Ehrenstein 111.

8. L. Curtius, *Die Wandmalerei Pompejis* (1929) 222ff.

9. F. Cumont, *After-Life in Roman Paganism* 96ff. According to Martial IV.3. the consecrated one is believed to dwell on the Bears, that is on the zenith of the celestial pole. Cf. Sauter (supra n. 4); V. Stegemann, *Astrologie und Universalgeschichte* 85ff. for the meaning of the constellations of the pole on Dionysus's celestial shield in Nonnos.

10. W. Weber, *Der Prophet und sein Gott* 77ff., 141ff. about the Alexander motif in Vergil's *Ecl.* IV. For the world-ruler oracle with regard to Augustus, see E. Norden, *Geburt d. Kindes* 159; idem 21, n.1 and F. Kampers, *Werdegang d. abendländ. Kaisermystik* 50.

11. G. Rodenwaldt, *AA* (1931) 334f.

The Hora of Spring

IN WELL-KNOWN NEO-ATTIC REPRESENTATIONS of the four Horae, each signifying a particular season by a different attribute, one Hora is accompanied by a little kid.[1] Her name has not been ascertained because it is not immediately clear whether she represents spring[2] or autumn.[3] From her position among the dancers, a position which changes from representation to representation, we cannot infer her significance. On the Campana plaques and the Berlin paste she is the leading figure. On the round altar from the Villa Albani she is the second behind the summer Hora, and she is second again on the Albani sarcophagus, but this time following her sister, the winter Hora. Thus, she must be identified by the gifts which she carries. But what are these attributes? The history of the Horae, who developed from nameless goddesses of growth to allegories of the seasons, indicates that their invention probably does not go back very far.[4] The style of the Campana plaques can hardly be earlier than the Augustan period.[5] Its association with classical models is obvious, even though real models of classical art were not actually copied. These Horae are new creations of their own time and their own artistic sphere. On the other hand, figures of the Ara Albani, because of their overly slender long limbs and high-belted garments, look more Hellenistic, although they are similar in bearing and general costumes to those on the terracotta plaques. They still seem to be connected with the late Hellenism that directly preceded them.[6] The mythical triad performing the dance of the Horae had already been given up in Alexandria during the reign of the Ptolemies, because the division of the year into four seasons with four goddesses corresponding to them had gradually become popular.[7] The differentiation of the goddesses could also have been invented at this time, just as the nine Muses were probably differentiated then.[8] But we still do not know what considerations led to the Horae acquiring their individual attributes.

According to a note by Athenaeus, one saw four Horae in a famous procession of Ptolemaios Philadelphos, ἑκάστη φέρουσα τοὺς ἰδίους καρπούς (each carrying her own fruits, V. 198a and b). This is the principle of almost all calendar pictures to this day. However, it is worth noting that the quotation indicates that the mythical concept of the goddesses had hardly been lost; as friendly beings of nature and bestowers of growth, each carries her own appropriate fruits. The number four brings to mind first of all that they signify seasons. The representation on the Neo-Attic Campana plaques goes very little beyond that. However, it broadens the concept of the καρποί (fruits); the Horae carry here not only fruit, but in a wider sense all the gifts which are characteristic for their season, including animals. Thereby, elements for the allegory of the seasons were created which were to remain valid for a long time. But the mythical source, an essential part of this ancient invention, is here still recognizable. It is still quite obvious on the Albani sarcophagus, where the same Horae bring their gifts for the wedding of Thetis, first as goddesses who participate in mythical events and only then as symbols of the seasons. In this case the winter Hora leads the way probably because the wedding month *Gamelion* belongs to her.[9] She shoulders a hare and ducks on a pole,[10] and drags a fat pig with her right hand.[11] These are her gifts. A mantle for bad weather and boots complete her outfit as a huntress.

Behind her comes the Hora with the kid which is easily recognized by its curved horns and shaggy fur. The Hora is wearing a long undergarment which slips somewhat off her right shoulder, and she casually carries a mantle over her left forearm. Her head, which is turned backwards, is wrapped in a scarf. C. Robert assumes that she carries fruit in the low bowl or basket in the palm of her hand, and accordingly identifies her as autumn.[12] E. Petersen has however already emphasized that the fruit does not justify such a precise designation. The identification becomes even less clear, since the last Hora in the row, who accordingly should personify spring, does not carry flowers in her dress but instead again carries fruit "like little apples."[13] The Campana plaques supply additional information for the solution of this problem. They show the same types only more completely and more precisely. The Hora who carries objects in her dress is here again present, but she is the next to the last figure, not the last. Her gifts are easy to recognize; she carries fruit among which are grapes and apples. Rohden and Winnefeld have recognized her correctly as the Hora of autumn. Therefore her sister, who is leading the dance, represents spring, and the order of the figures on the Campana plaques is spring, summer, autumn, winter. On the Albani sarcophagus, using the same reasoning, the order of the figures is winter, spring, summer and autumn.[14]

Consequently the Hora of spring in Neo-Attic representations, whom we can definitely identify on the Campana plaques and probably again on the Albani sarcophagus is distinguished by four characteristics. A loosely wrapped cloak and a scarf around her head are part of her costume. Her attribute on the sarcophagus is a little he-goat; on the Campana plaques, a tiny kid.[15] Also she carries a flat, dish-like utensil in her hand, which, compared with others of its kind, is most likely a basket filled with flowers. The "capretto" is a gift of spring; it is an attribute that can be added to the fruit of the season in the same way as the flowers in the basket. The costume though is a different matter, especially the head-cloth that is worn like a cap. Since this cloth is rendered traditionally in different ways, its meaning is less easily understood than that of the other attributes. The artist of the round altar has omitted it altogether, and on the terracotta plaques it is pleated. It belonged apparently only to the Hora of spring.[16] Certainly only she wears it on the Albani sarcophagus and on the Arretine cup, and there it is more like a cap which covers the hair and chignon. It could not have served as protection against bad weather which could be possible were the winter Hora to wear it. We must derive its meaning from different associations, and indeed it may be possible to trace these new connections.

The strange form of the headdress that the Hora of spring wears on the Campana plaques is not unknown. It is the very headdress which appears in numerous representations from Hellenistic times on, worn by women during a sacrifice. It is pleated like the one that the pious old woman wears on the Vienna bronze statuette published by J. Bankò.[17] Moreover, we know the kind of sacrifice in which women who wore this special headdress participated. The same connection between rustic costumes and the performance of Dionysiac celebrations, which W. Amelung established in regard to the knotted coat of the Vienna bronze and similar representations, also holds for the cap-like headdress.[18] On sarcophagi the nurses of mythical heroines, Phaedra for instance or Medea, wear it as part of their rustic dress,[19] just as the women from the Spreewald region in East Germany do nowadays. The drunken old woman of the Munich Glyptothek wears it, certainly, as a peasant woman. However, it also has Dionysiac associations. Around Rome it was occasionally worn by maenads who participated in rustic as well as Dionysian celebrations.[20] Mainly it belongs to the representation of Dionysian sacrifices as on the Arretine cup with the birth of Dionysus[21] or on the significant sarcophagi which Bankò[22] and Amelung[23] have already discussed. The sarcophagi are especially interesting with regard to our question. At the end of a mythical Bacchic representation of the *thiasos*, each sarcophagus has a little group of women, one of whom sacrifices chickens; this is a real offering in contrast to the poetic-mythical world of the rest of the representation. Dionysus whose statue is always shown, is the recipient of the sacrifice. He is portrayed not as the enraptured youth, but instead is bearded and wears a long robe. He is the Dionysus of the mysteries whose most characteristic attributes are the *polos* and *tympanon*. The religious conception of this sphere becomes ambiguous and it is in a curious way evident in the figure of Dionysus. On the sarcophagus of the Galleria dei Candelabri in the Vatican (Fig. 1) Dionysus is attended by Silenus, his mystagogue, in appearance an itinerant philosopher.[24] Next to Silenus there is a ram, the animal of Sabazius.[25] The pine tree in whose shade the statue is set up also belongs to Sabazius.[26] The same god is portrayed on the fragment of a sarcophagus in the Villa Albani (Fig. 2) where remainders of the Dionysian cult scene still exist—the old woman with the headdress in front of the altar, a dancing satyr with a wineskin on his shoulders. Nevertheless, the statue of the god on its garlanded pedestal is this time priapic, which is sufficiently manifested by the folds of the garment. He is here also furnished with the big cymbal of the mythic cult. On another sarcophagus in Genoa (Fig. 3), a satyr again brings Dionysus the leaping he-goat, his proper sacrificial animal. This constitutes a transition, as it were, from the representation of a real sacrifice to the mythical conception of the *thiasos*. On these monuments women always perform the sacrifice, the actual offering before the cult image, and the one who sacrifices is always covered with the cap-like headdress.[27]

Into such a circle of sacrificing women we can place now on the basis of her costume the beautiful invention which we recognize in Neo-Attic representations as the Hora of spring. She is none other than a participant in a rustic feast. Covered with the cap of the sacrificing woman she brings a he-goat or little kid as her gift. By now it is certain that the animal is not only the characteristic gift of spring, but above all

Fig. 1. Sarcophagus with a Dionysian sacrifice, detail, Rome, Musei Vaticani

Fig. 2. Fragment of sarcophagus with a Dionysian celebration, Rome, Villa Albani

Fig. 3. Sarcophagus with a Dionysian sacrifice, detail, Genoa, Palazzo Bianco

Fig. 4. Month of March, *Die Calender-bilder des Chronographen von 354*, R1-Barb. lat. 2154, Rome, Biblioteca Vaticana

the animal of the Dionysian feasts, just as the cap is an understandable attribute of Dionysian festivities. As the monuments show, women, particularly, participate in Dionysian rites. Moreover, these rites are for the most part festivals of spring; this applies to the Attic *Dionysia* as well as the Roman *Liberalia* of March 17, and perhaps the representation of the just mentioned sarcophagi is related to them.[28] Indeed quite a different principle emerges than the one used in the Ptolemaic procession where the Horae of the seasons are endowed with their καρποί. The Hora of spring of the Neo-Attic artists carries not only her symbols, but she appears at certain feasts as only one of the large number of women who celebrate Dionysus.[29] Only then can the he-goat or kid and cap be really accounted for. The season is thereby described by its characteristic cult.

This is also precisely the principle of the Attic calendar of feasts. The actor who brings the Dionysian he-goat along in the month *Elaphebolion* has the same meaning, and it was in accordance with this principle of a calendar of feasts that the Neo-Attic Hora of spring was invented and endowed with her attributes. The idea that an old calendar existed in Rome with exactly this kind of picture has been repeatedly discussed.[30] In the chronograph of 354 A.D. the picture of March is still a satyr with a leaping he-goat (Fig. 4).[31] The image remained the same and attempts were continually made to renew its poetic content, even though its true origin had been forgotten long ago.

Notes

1. For examples and illustrations see the following works. Albani sarcophagus, C. Robert, *Die Sarkophagreliefs* II pl. 1; Campana reliefs, H. von Rohden and H. Winnefeld, *Architekton. römische Tonreliefs*, 1911, pls. 57, 98; Albani round altar, *EA* 3298; Berlin paste, A. Furtwängler, *Berlin Katal.* 6262; Arretine cup, H. Dragendorff, "Terra sigillata," *BonnJbb* 96 (1895) 64ff. Likewise A. Oxé, *Arretin. Reliefgef.* pls. 32, 34, 78ff.
2. E. Petersen, "Sepolcro di Via Latina," *AdI* (1861) 208ff. Rohden-Winnefeld, *op. cit.* text 89ff.
3. P. Herrmann, *De Horarum apud veteres figuris*, diss. (Berlin, 1887) 31, n. 3. Robert, *op.cit.* 3f. F. Hauser, *Die Neuatt. Relig.* 103.
4. *MythLex* 2729ff., s.v. "Horai." Later on, esp. on sarcophagi, the allegory is also represented by winged boys and erotes with gifts of the seasons besides the Horai. Petersen, *op.cit.* 215ff.
5. Likewise Rohden-Winnefeld, *op. cit.* 91.
6. Hauser, *op.cit.*, includes them therefore in his second "Alexandrine" group.
7. Herrmann, *op.cit.* 12, 32.
8. O. Bie, *Die Musen* 105; cf. *MythLex* s.v. "Musen."
9. Robert, *ibid.* Rohden-Winnefeld, *ibid.* 91f., see pl. 47. Both authors identify the same scene on Campana plaques mentioning only the winter Hora.
10. Thus the centaur traditionally shoulders the killed hare as was already shown on the Françoise Vase, *FR* I 3; Chiron as guest at the wedding of Thetis.
11. In a later development, the narrative elements join these attributes as on the mosaic of Schebba, *AA* (1903) 99, Inv. Mos. II, 86. Here the pig is presented running free beside the winter Hora and a man is shown gathering olives. The comparison of the ages is added, cf. F. Boll, *NJbb* 31 (1903) 103; consequently the seasons age like man, but nothing like this is yet noticeable on Neo-Attic monuments. Thus, the material gradually accumulates for the allegory which was logically completed only during the Middle Ages. At Chartres Cathedral winter is an old man, December slaughters a pig, E. Houvet, *Chartres* II, North Portal 88, 90; the slaughter of pigs belongs therefore to the

typical descriptions of the month of December as on the Saturn woodcut by Sebald Beham, see F. Boll and C. Bezold, *Sternglaube* 49, pl. 6, fig. 12.

12. C. Robert, *AdI* (1861) 211.
13. Robert, *ibid.*, from a note by F. Matz.
14. Likewise on the glass paste where, however, winter is missing. On the round Albani pedestal which renders the attributes altogether more casually, the spring and summer Hora were apparently mistaken for each other; a year with the order of summer, spring, winter, autumn is hardly possible. A similar error occurred on the Arretine cup. Oxé, *ibis.* incorrectly called the summer Hora, with a wreath and branch of poppy, spring, autumn with fruit, summer, and the Hora with the kid again autumn.
15. The same holds for the Hora of spring on Pompeian walls, Herrmann, *ibid.* 39, *Museo Naz. Naples,* 14, pl. 32. Cf. the Horae from the Casa degli amorini dorati, *NSc* (1905) 133 and T. Warscher, *Pompeji* (Berlin, 1925) 193–96. Unfortunately photographs are missing but one can recognize the same types from the description.
16. Contrary to Rohden and Winnefeld, *ibid.* 90; I doubt whether the Hora of winter, on the plaques with the seasons, had any kind of headdress at all. Only single locks appear here whereas on the plaques with the bull, the same figure definitely wears a tight cap, at least on some examples, *ibid.* pl. 47.
17. J. Bankò, *ÖJh* (1919) 296ff., pl. 6.
18. W. Amelung, *Die Sculpturen des Vatican. Museums* I 698.
19. Bankò, *op.cit.* 297, n. 3.
20. Round pedestal in the Museo Naz. Romano, *NSc* 33 (1908) 446.
21. *Brit. Mus., Catal. of Roman Pottery,* 27, fig. 21.
22. *Ibid.* 298, n. 10.
23. See sarcophagus fragm., R. Gostkowski, *Eos* (1928) 321ff. M. Bieber, *JdI* 32 (1917) 38ff.
24. From photograph by F. Faraglia.
25. *MythLex* 252, s.v. "Sabazios"; for the connection between concepts of Sabazios and Dionysiac ideas, see F. Cumont, *Die oriental. Relig.* (1931) 316, 25. On some sarcophagi, e.g., one in Genova, Pal. Bianco (Fig. 3) this Dionysus outwardly resembles, as far as costume and appearance are concerned, the statue of Sardanapalus in the Vatican; L. Curtius pointed out his connection with Sabazios, *JdI* 43 (1928) 281ff.
26. *MythLex, ibid.* 256.
27. As on the fragment published by Gostkowski (supra n. 23) a cloak, pulled over the head, occasionally replaces the scarf; it is similar to the *capitis velatio* which is commonly used for a Roman sacrifice.
28. Gostkowski, *ibid.* (supra n. 23) 328.
29. In poetic literature Horae themselves lead festivals, esp. Dionysiac ones; cf. *MythLex* 2730, s.v. "Horai."
30. L. Deubner, *Attische Feste* 248. P. Herrmann, *Diss.* 41, recognized correctly the connection between the kid and Dionysiac ideas. However, he related the kid, at least for the Neo-Attic reliefs with the Horae, not to spring but to autumn. Wine and grapes, the gifts of Bacchus, are indeed those of autumn as soon as one identifies each season by her gifts, following the other principle of their allegory. This second way of identifying was also used early, see Ovid, *Metam.* II.27ff., where autumn has Dionysiac features. Later these ideas become more and more conspicuous, e.g. on the above mentioned mosaic of Schebba (supra n. 11) 97ff. where autumn appears like a female Dionysus accompanied by a panther and pouring wine from a kantharos. On the Concordier monument at Boretto, *NSc* 8 (1932) 177, spring is shown with a suckling goat.
31. J. Strzygowski, "Die Calenderbilder des Chronographen von 354," *JdI* (1888) 1. Erg. Heft, pls. 20, 21, and 62ff. Bibl. Barberini, Rome. A look at the dress of Mars shows that an earlier model was used but misunderstood. The tetrastich calls for a wolf's fur. The cloven hoof, however, which the picture clearly shows, does not belong to a wolf but to the he-goat's fur of the satyr, who was its original wearer.

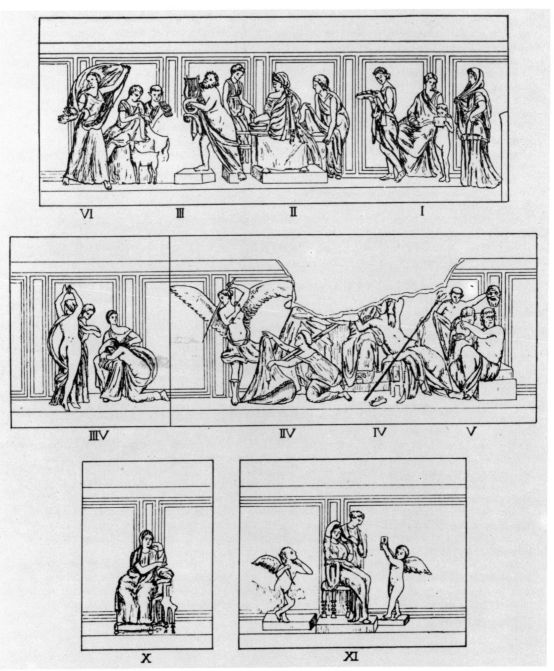

Fig. 1. Schematic drawing, Frieze, Villa of the Mysteries, Pompeii

The Great Frieze in
the Villa of the Mysteries

The VILLA OF THE MYSTERIES, located outside the city walls of Pompeii toward the northwest, takes its name from the great frieze that covers the walls of an "oecus," a kind of lounge. This frieze is doubtless the most important ancient painting still in existence; it is also one of the most enigmatic.*

The astonishing series of twenty-nine life-sized figures (Fig. 1), lined up before a strictly rhythmical, painted wall architecture of the so-called Second Roman-Campanian Style, poses more questions than can as yet be answered. For more than sixty years discussion has been going on concerning the artistic origin, the purpose, and especially the meaning of these magnificent paintings. Nevertheless—and despite all previous attempts and partial successes, attained mainly through research of recent years—the pictorial world of the frieze appears more puzzling than ever. Complete analyses such as those undertaken by M. Bieber in 1928 and by L. Curtius one year later hardly seem to lie within our reach. There are still too many questions about details which must be answered. Thus, this essay will have to limit itself to particular points concerning the great whole. Two of them—actually two of the most significant—will form the primary objects of our attention: the fleeing girl at the left corner of the long wall, and the winged, striking figure near the right corner of the shorter back wall of the rectangular hall.[1]

The description of the villa itself and its building history are not under discussion here. Only one important circumstance should be recalled briefly. As is known, R. Herbig successfully demonstrated some time ago that the walls of the room, as well as the arrangement of the windows and doors, had the same appearance when the painters of the frieze started their work as they have today. The frieze has not been damaged by later rebuildings. It was planned for the architectural conditions that have remained to this day. The calculated centralization of the rear wall, with the group of deities in the middle, points quite clearly to this (Fig. 9). Furthermore, it seems that the painted architecture preceded the frieze. The figures hardly take it into account, and the perspective socle had to be added in order to provide a base for them. When, at a later date, a portico was constructed as a roofed outside gallery around the building, the already existing large south window was taken into consideration by widening the position of the portico columns so that the light coming in from the terrace would not be diminished. The frieze was to remain clearly visible. In any case, the room was well provided with daylight and was easily accessible. Nothing in the architectural design points at a secret to be guarded.[2]

THE LEFT LONG WALL (Fig. 2)

We shall now turn to the figures. A young woman has just entered (Fig. 3). Perhaps
we should assume that she passed through the same little door used by today's
visitor. In any case, her still lingering step indicates the direction of the frieze. Our
eyes follow hers. The entering woman is certainly an important person, perhaps an
initiate, ͵α μύστης, as she is often called. She is dressed in a very peculiar way. With
her long, double-belted peplos and her head covered with a shawl, the end of which
she lifts with her left hand, she is a conspicuous rarity in the history of Roman
costume. She represents a precious anachronism, emphasized by the unusual way in
which her other hand rests on her right hip—an uncommon pose for a Roman
woman with dignified gait. Yet there are many oddities of costume in this part of the
frieze, most of them still unexplained. We have to leave these questions as they are
for the time being. At most one could add that the color of the peplos worn by the
veiled woman probably should be called white, even though the local color is tinted
by shadows. This feature may have a pertinent meaning. The white garment of the
initiate or, rather, of already initiated members seems to have played a role in
various ancient mysteries.[3]

It is time, however, to raise another, more pressing question. Into what kind of
company does the veiled lady really enter? To this question is tied a very simple
methodical consideration which is by no means new but which seems to me not
always sufficiently noted. I am thinking of the following, obvious fact. The persons
who move side by side in this frieze do not all belong to the same sphere of reality.
Some of them apparently stand on our side of human reality, the normal one, as it
were. They might do things or find themselves in situations which we do not immediately understand because they are unfamiliar to us. Nevertheless, it is clear that
in their strange conduct and unusual behavior, they neither do nor indicate anything
which under similar circumstances could not be done or experienced by other human
beings. They are inhabitants of the realm of our common human reality. The
woman who has just entered belongs with them. In contrast, however, there are
other beings who are not depicted as less real, but who nonetheless are not of the
same nature. They are part of an otherworldly reality, fictitious, mythological, or
poetic. Silens and satyrs, even the gods in the center of the back wall, are not real in
the same sense as the human beings in the frieze are. Only in art, which itself is invention, can the representatives of these two worlds meet so easily, without reserva-
tions. But this is saying too much. Not in every art will both spheres of reality, the
natural and the intellectual, blend so smoothly. In Greek votive reliefs, to name but
one example, gods and human beings also confront each other. Nevertheless, they
remain separated. Art has the means to make the distinction visible, and it emphasizes the separation instead of cancelling it. In the frieze of the Villa of the Mysteries,
men and mythological beings associate on equal footing without any hesitation,
even with a degree of naturalness. In this I recognize a Roman characteristic. The
same tendency to mix both sides of reality is expressed in Latin literature as well.
Thus Horace says of himself that "the dances of the light-footed nymphs with the

satyrs" separate him from the "vulgar throng."[4] This is not merely a poetic form of speech; it is meant to be a concrete illustration, just as is our frieze. But precisely because this is so, and because the work of art allows the observer to forget the distinction so easily, it is necessary to ask anew, to which of the two worlds does each figure of this frieze belong?

The wistful lady who has just entered is certainly a real person. Thus she belongs to this side of reality, our worldly sphere. The path she is about to take leads past several more or less clearly separated groups. The first, apparently not noticed by the veiled woman, is comprised of a seated woman and a boy reading. It has long been known that the reading itself signifies a religious act, one for which there is other evidence.[5] At the moment nothing new can be added to what has been established. It might be relevant, however, to recall that we do not know what the boy is reading. A prayer, a sacred text—these and other possibilites remain open. A sacred formula into which the name of the arriving person is inserted must also be considered; we know from inscriptions the great importance that was attributed to personal names in the mysteries.[6] Be that as it may, the point is that the group is involved in an entrance rite, an *introitus*. That much is obvious from its position within the whole composition. In the course of the frieze it represents a preparatory and probably a subordinate episode.

Then follows the sacrificial rite, if one can call it so. The young girl with the silver platter is probably part of it, although she is separated from the main action by a small space. The mantle wound around her hip is significant. We probably know the ancient name of this garb: it is called κατάζωσις.[7] Acolytes, male and female, often wear it in sacrificial scenes on Dionysiac monuments. Thus the girl so dressed is one of the assistants; I would call her an ἐπιθύουσα. The sacrificial group (Figs. 2–4), then, consists of four persons. Three are apparently acolytes. Only one, the seated woman who wears a beautiful headdress and a cloak knotted on the left shoulder (the *palladium quadratum*), carries out the ritual attended by the others. She functions as priestess. Unfortunately, not much can be seen of the sacrifice. Even less can be explained. The scene of the ritual is an offering table. The objects that the acolyte carries in on the silver platter are difficult to make out, though they might be loaves of bread. In any case, the sacrifice is not a blood offering. A servant girl who is bending over comes next. She is the only member of the group who is not adorned with an olive wreath. It is significant that the priestess is seated, for sitting during the sacrifice is not the rule. In this respect she is similar to the seated figure who stirs a concoction in the crater placed beside her in the sacrificial scene on a sarcophagus in the Villa Medici (Fig. 5). The priestess in the Villa of the Mysteries seems to have grasped an object from the shallow basket offered to her from the left. With her left hand she lifts the concealing cloth. The object taken from the shallow container was probably the same little twig that is now being sprinkled from a small pitcher held by the helper on the right, who wears a mantle wound around her hip like the girl who carries in the platter. The liquid being poured cannot be determined because water, as well as wine—even milk—could be involved.[8] It is also possible that the action ran in the opposite direction and that the twig will be returned to the covered platter

Fig. 2. Frieze, detail, the long left wall, Fig. 1 (I-IV)

Fig. 3. Frieze, detail, Fig. 1 (I)

Fig. 4. Frieze, detail, Fig. 1 (II)

Fig. 5. Sarcophagus with sacrifice, Rome, Villa Medici

after this ceremony. The fact that the principal person turns her back to the observer adds to the mystery of the undertaking. One has the impression that something is happening but that no word is being spoken nor anything explained. Apparently there is no known Bacchic ritual which completely corresponds to this act, nor do other mysteries offer precise parallels.[9]

Nevertheless, from this preliminary description a more certain fact is revealed which will prove important for the further study of the frieze. Up to this point we have dealt with actions and actors belonging to the world of human reality. But if one advances only one step, one enters a different world. The border of our side of reality is then overstepped. Directly behind, though turned away from the group that performs the sacrifice, stands the singing silen (Fig. 6).

The transition into the mythical world happens abruptly, without preparation; the composition takes no notice of it at all. Silenus's right leg overlaps a considerable portion of the acolyte with the pitcher who stands next to him. Although they are not equally real, both figures move within the same real space. The acolyte stands somewhat in the background, while the silen, broadly drawn, is distinctly a foreground figure. He is almost naked, and no longer a youth. His cloak slips down from his hip. He has propped his nine-stringed lyre on a stone pillar, as was customary in a musical performance.[10] Moreover, he rests his left foot on the low plinth of the pillar as if to rush forward; this too is not uncommon. His pose is that of a singer who, thrusting forward, follows the power of his own voice while his body swings back and forth to the rhythm of the music. At the same time, he accompanies himself on his stringed instrument. Tannhäuser sang this way, according to the old tradition of Bayreuth. Our silen too is a kind of magic singer, his snub-nosed face and bald head, framed by an olive wreath and sparse gray hair, lifted toward heaven—ecstatic. The whole figure, but especially the face, is one of the triumphs of ancient painting which has survived. One must go as far as Raphael's *Parnassus* to find its equal. In both cases the legend *numine afflatus* would be in order because that is obviously the meaning of the whole conception. This silen does not represent a drunkard similar to Falstaff (as a silen sometimes does), but a singing seer comparable to the one in Vergil's Sixth Eclogue, which was written shortly after the frieze of the mysteries was painted.[11] Intoxicated he is, although hardly from wine. The wise silen here becomes an artist. Rare insight and the magic of music are consolidated into words and sounds in his song. In the context of the frieze, this figure represents the first allusion to the Dionysiac sphere of *enthusiasmos*, the first modality of Bacchic madness, the μανία of the sage, of the singer, of art.[12]

The scenes change very fast. Alongside the silen, a small rock rises from the ground like a stage set-piece (Figs. 2, 7, 8), in the middle of the room, as it were. It is somewhat surprising because thus far there has not been any hint of a definite locality. In front of the rock stands a small goat, while on it sits a young female creature who nurses a kid. Her companion holds a syrinx. For the explanation of this group, earlier research may be cited.[13] The three following points may be made in summary. These creatures with pointed ears are certainly not ordinary human beings. Rather, they belong to the family of satyrs, and therefore they are fictional

Fig. 6. Frieze, detail, Fig. 1 (III)

Fig. 7. Frieze, detail, Fig. 1 (III)

characters, members of the bizarre court of Bacchus. Secondly, they form a self-contained group. Silenus does not notice them nor they him. That much is still recognizable even though, toward the silen, the lower contour of the group is not well enough preserved to be seen clearly. Thirdly, it should be mentioned that an old Dionysiac reminiscence, like the suckling of the kid, is turned here into a Hellenistic rustic idyl with shepherd and shepherdess, a satyr-boy and a satyr-girl, as guardians of the flock of goats in rocky isolation, in no one's company but their own.[14] The relationship between bucolic poetry and Bacchic features is well known, and also becomes evident here. In this case, although the satyr children take the place of the shepherd couple, the basic situation stays Bacchic. It remains doubtful whether any meaningful relationship exists between the silen and the satyr children. Both represent Dionysiac elements, but each acts independently. Possibly the situation can be compared to song and theme: also in Vergil the silen starts his song in a way his audience does not expect, with cosmic enigmas such as the origin of the world, the elements, and the seasons, all part of a friendly pastoral idyl.[15] In addition, the question arises whether in the two forms of music before us a contrast is not being deliberately shown between the noble lyre and the rustic syrinx; in other words, between the sublime style of inspired song and the simple manner of a pastoral tune. The miracle of inspiration belongs to a higher level, to that of Silenus.[16]

With this, however, ends the Bacchic following. We are not granted much time for meditation because suddenly a human being, with a sharp outcry, as it were, bursts into the mythical idyl. This time it is a much disturbed real person, a fleeing girl.

THE FLEEING GIRL (Fig. 8)

She is clearly a foreground figure. Her right leg already covers part of the pastoral group while she, striding out, seems to run obliquely from her left toward the edge of the painted platform. Thus one can see her entire form, like a statue, without any overlapping. She is the last figure on the left long side of the frieze; looking back, her glance is directed toward the corner of the short rear wall.

One sees a young female, dressed rather lightly and wearing her hair in the so-called melon coiffure, a common Hellenistic fashion. Her long chiton is hardly more than an undergarment and is supplemented by a cloak which she holds above her head from behind. It might be more accurate here to use the Latin terms *tunica* and *pallium*. The sleeveless chiton is white and without any ornament.

It is generally assumed that the girl is running away frightened and terrified. Even the face with the half-opened mouth seems to express alarm. There can be little doubt about the interpretation since the iconography of this action of fear is well known; it can be traced back to the art of classical Greece. Pulling a cloak, or even the upper part of the peplos, over the head is a first reaction when a woman is afraid or feels pursued—as if such a delicate garment could hide or protect her when no other refuge offers itself.[17] The problem of this figure lies therefore not in her pose, which is easily explained, but in the question why is the girl frightened, from what does she flee?

Fig. 8. Frieze, detail, Fig. 1 (IV)

So far, this question has been answered mainly in two different ways. In the first, the girl is afraid of the unveiling of the phallus which is under way at the opposite end of the rear wall (Figs. 9, 10);[18] or, in the second, she is frightened by the beating scene, represented in the same corner of the rear wall and continuing on the adjacent long wall on the other side of the room (Figs. 10, 14).[19] Both these answers share the disadvantage that they accept a much larger space between the effect represented and its cause—a space filled with other painted scenes—than would be natural for such a representation; the frightened girl is on the left end and the proposed reason for her terror near the corresponding corner on the opposite side. Additional hypotheses must be introduced in order to explain this anomaly. The most widely held supposition is that the entire frieze is a copy of an older original, and that the copyists adapted it to the architecture of the room at the request of the patrons by placing details differently or by omissions and unjustified additions.[20] On this assumption, any shifting in the sequence of the various scenes of the frieze can obviously be justified with complete freedom; thus one can, for instance, suggest that the fleeing girl originally belonged to the scene of the unveiling of the phallus. Clearly it is an arbitrary procedure which is more likely to dissolve the data of the ancient monument than to explain them. The hypothesis that the entire frieze is a copy is possible but not proven, and all suggestions to correct it through pertinent ancient evidence are up to this time inconclusive. Under these circumstances the best thing would be to follow, so to speak, a *petitio principii*, a philological method for dealing with an ancient text. That means making emendations only after all other possibilities for a significant explanation have been exhausted. In my opinion the interpretation of the frieze of the mysteries has not reached such a critical state. The possibilities of an explanation on the basis of the data have by no means been treated fully.

The beating scene will have to be considered later by itself. First it is necessary to ask once more for the actual reasons to link the fleeing girl on the left to the phallus ceremony at the right end of the short rear wall. We can harldy maintain that the composition itself recommends such a combination. If the fleeing girl is tentatively transferred to the open side of the liknon group, opposite the kneeling girl, where perhaps she could be placed, she would obviously move toward the supposed object of her terror instead of away from it. This would mean not only that the figure is incorrectly put into its present place, but also that it is shown in reverse. A similar objection might be raised to the psychological argument which has often been advanced in order to prove that the fleeing girl and the liknon group belong together, namely, that the young woman is afraid of the phallus. The question is whether the argument itself can be sufficiently based on authentic ancient statements. It is obvious that by referring to a social-psychological motive, modern views and modes of feeling can play a part which must not necessarily be ascribed to the ancient artist and his public. If, for instance, the liknon scene represents a genuine ceremony of mysteries to be actually performed, then the question would remain whether the behavior of the fleeing girl at that moment represents a likely and altogether admissible reaction, in other words, if it is motivated by the cult itself.[21] It is not impossible that this is so, but it would at least have to be demonstrated in a credible way. As

Fig. 9. Frieze of the rear wall, Fig. 1 (V-VII)

Fig. 10. Frieze, detail, Fig. 1 (VII)

a matter of fact, the flight from the phallus would not be without precedent as an ancient subject. We have representations of young women fleeing from a phallic symbol in late archaic and early classical art.[22] We must ask here, however, to what kind of reality or conception these older images were related. Of those we know, not one represents a sacred rite. Therefore none can be used to support the suggestion—against the well-established data of the monument—that the fleeing girl be added to the phallus scene in the Pompeian frieze of the mysteries.

THE LIKNON SCENE (Fig. 10)

Some considerations of a more general nature have to be added here regarding the unveiling scene at the right end of the rear wall. The group does not only puzzle the modern observer, since the *pentimenti*, more numerous here than elsewhere, show that even the ancient painter faced difficulties.[23] Moreover, the upper part of the group unfortunately has been destroyed. Nevertheless, it can be stated that it consisted of three women, one kneeling in the foreground and two others standing behind her. One of these, approaching from the left, carries an offering plate. She and the kneeling girl turn their backs on the divine couple, which could easily mean that the girls are unaware of the gods, that only the viewer can perceive them, whereas they remain invisible to the persons who are represented.[24] The kneeling girl wears the previously mentioned cloak that is knotted around the hips. A torch rests on her left shoulder indicating that the ceremony takes place at night. She leans forward toward the liknon which, as usual, is represented as a longish basket with a border that rises gradually backward in a curved line. With the right hand she grasps the purple cloth that covers the erect object in the basket. Her left hand is raised slightly above this object, most likely in order to lift the cloth. The unveiling is under way but has not yet taken place. The covered object can hardly be anything but the phallus symbol—to be expected in this setting—in spite of its uncommon, straight upper line. It has indeed always been explained this way. After all, in representation of Bacchic rites—and this scene is one—liknon and phallus belong together.[25]

This last-mentioned fact calls again for a brief comment. The combination of liknon and phallus is well documented by monuments at least since the first century B.C. The same applies to the veiling and unveiling of the symbol in the liknon; it is well to be mindful, however, that all modern knowledge of these actions is based on visual observation, that is, on interpretation of pictorial representations. The possible sources of error in this method, forced upon us by ancient evidence, need hardly be stated. Another question is what special significance we can ascribe to these symbols in known Bacchic mythology. There can be no doubt that they are part of the Bacchic sphere of symbols, although this is by no means self-evident. In its practical use, the liknon is a winnowing basket, and therefore an implement that serves in Demeter's or Ceres' cultivation of the fields, but not in the cultivation of vines. In fact, the cult of Dionysos Liknites, in which the agricultural corn shovel was connected with Dionysus not only by its myth but also literally by its descriptive name was earlier affiliated with an ancient cult of the earth goddess.[26] Originally bread and wine belonged to separate religious practices, just as different agricultural conditions underlie their cultivation. This fact has always been remembered, even in their common cult.

The question about the meaning of the phallus symbol probably must be asked in a similar way. In an agrarian cult it is not difficult to understand the male symbol as a necessary prerequisite of, or supplement to, female fertility personified by a maternal earth goddess. Actually it seems that in classical times it was mainly associated as a ritual symbol with feminine religions, either in cults that were dedicated to an earth or grain goddess, such as the Eleusinian Demeter, or in sacred rites that were, according to their statutes, performed by women, such as the rituals of the Attic Thesmophorai.[27] In both cases we have reasons to assume that objects in the form of a phallus were part of the ritual. The cults also have in common the secret character of the ritual. Thus the phallus symbol in the liknon—or in any other "bread basket"—appears as the pictorial representation of a logical and natural thought. All this, however, does not apply to the Bacchic religion in the same way. How bread and wine came together in that sphere is still uncertain. Dionysus himself is not a phallic god in all his numerous pictorial representations as was, for instance, Pan or Hermes. On the other hand, he was surrounded from early times by the phallus-happy satyrs and the thyrsos-wielding maenads who made up his mythical attendants. In this context, however, something else should be remembered. Maenads and satyrs, though they are both Dionysiac creatures, by no means always appear as good friends. Just the opposite is true. As is well known, there are numerous representations of maenads who successfully resist the obtrusive satyrs in a rather straightforward way. They disapprove of phallic conduct, or rather misconduct[28] and on the whole show a dislike for the masculine. Hence Pentheus and Orpheus became the enemies and victims of the frenzied women. From these considerations, which by the way are not new, two conclusions that may be of importance for the following section might be drawn regarding the assessment of phallic symbols in the religion of Dionysus. We must always take into account that in this circle the phallus image can assume an unfriendly connotation, that is to say, a recollection of an original antagonism between the sexes or, more accurately, the female's hostility toward the male. We have no examples of representations, except relatively late ones, which give the male symbol any other than its natural meaning, nor of any which bestow an esoteric or beneficial character on the unveiling ritual. Older phallus images of the Dionysiac iconography represent phallic creatures and mythical situations, possibly also phallus processions, but no mysteries.

ONCE AGAIN: THE FLEEING GIRL (Fig. 8)

To deny to the liknon scene (Fig. 10) of the Pompeian frieze the character of a cult ritual will not be possible. This interpretation is supported by the fact that the women who participate in it are identified as human beings—and not as mythical personages—by their costume and demeanor. Not much has yet been gained from the preceding considerations toward an explanation of the fleeing girl at the opposite corner (Figs. 8, 9). However the discussion has failed to support the theory that the girl belongs to the liknon group. It is time to return to this problem now and, if possible, to come to a decision.

Two monuments which for a long time have been important in this discussion have not yet been mentioned. Quite obviously both belong to the sphere of problems confronting us here. It is not at all clear, however, what they can contribute to the solution of these problems. The Campana relief with the fleeing winged woman has already been compared correctly by Bieber since it too shows the phallus, this time uncovered, in a winnowing basket (Fig. 11).[29] A half-naked female figure kneels behind the basket, touching it with her right hand; with the raised left hand she seems to seize the winged woman by one end of her cloak. She is perhaps to be understood as a maenad, definitely not as a priestess, for behind her stands an ithyphallic satyr who, with his left hand apparently pleading, supports her efforts to induce the winged woman to stay.

It is obvious that the latter escapes from the liknon and its contents; her rejecting gesture removes any doubt, yet the rest cannot be explained with enough certainty. Not only the name of the winged creature but also the meaning of the entire representation is under discussion. None of the already suggested explanations of either an allegorical or a speculative nature has so far done justice to all the details. We have no pictorial reference for a winged personification of Aidos, a conjecture first suggested by Winckelmann.[30] To recognize this figure as Dike or the star-virgin Astraea would justify her wings but not her action.[31] After all, what business have these three personages among the satyrs? I doubt that the question has yet been answered in a satisfactory way.

Another possible interpretation has been hardly considered, one which would have the advantage of being simple in comparison to those which involve allegory or mystery. I believe that the Campana relief illustrates a mythical story, the tale of Iris' visit to the satyrs. The same moment is represented on the Brygos cup in London where, her mission completed, Iris turns away in horror while the obtrusive followers of Dionysus still try to hold her by her garment—in vain.[32] The Roman terracotta relief is clearly at the end of a long pictorial tradition. In addition to the correspondences between the cup and the relief, the differences are also interesting. Dionysus, whom Brygos still showed present, is missing on the relief. The phallus appears in a two-fold meaning, as sexual member and as symbol in the winnowing basket. The latter pictorial symbol is a Hellenistic-Roman contribution. It still preserves, however, the older Dionysiac power, at the same time aggressive and defensive, and a thorn in the side of Hera's messenger.

If, as I believe, the Campana relief goes back to this story, it can add little more than a remote mythical analogy to the understanding of the completely different, cultic liknon group in the frieze of the mysteries. It remains to be investigated how important it is as such, especially in connection with the flagellation group to be discussed later. This myth can hardly be considered as binding evidence for the explanation of the fleeing girl as a human figure. The girl shows natural horror and fear which differ from the self-conscious sentiments of aversion, rejection, and utmost condemnation which the daughter of heaven shows as she leaves the satyrs behind.

The second monument, the Roman mosaic from Djemila (Fig. 12), which recently has been cited several times in the discussion about the fleeing girl, also needs further critical investigation.[33] Its appearance indicates that it belongs in the sphere of the other relevant monuments. The phallus in the liknon, the kneeling girl who uncovers it, and this time also the moment of the disclosure itself are distinctly represented. In addition, the demonstration of the symbol is directed toward the maidenly figure to the right in front of the liknon, who clearly rejects it, just as on the Campana relief. She is certainly not winged, as F. Matz has already noticed.[34] The parallel to the fleeing girl of the frieze is nevertheless not complete, because the figure on the mosaic is not fleeing; nor does she belong typologically to the series of fleeing women who protect themselves with a veil-like fluttering garment held from behind over their head. Instead she is doing something quite different: she dances, and the vehemence of her dance is indicated by her loose hair and the ends of the garment which flutter around her. Maenads dance like this and we must understand her to be one of them. Her bare leg also fits the common Roman conception of a maenad. The horror which her eloquent hands express is like a pantomime performed by a trained ballet dancer. The entire picture is one of four Dionysiac scenes which are distributed on the four sides of the mosaic pavement. Among them is the sacrifice of the pious king Ikarios, who received the gift of viticulture from the god of wine and gave it a home in Attica.[35] Perhaps this maenad too should be given a mythical name. A contrast between her and the seated woman was certainly intended. We might have to look for it in the maenadic frenzy associated with contempt for men, as was the case with the Minyades and the daughters of Cadmos. Her opposite, the quietly seated woman, then, appears as the domestic matron, and the *tabellae* which she grasps could be her marriage contract usually held by the bride on contemporary Roman marriage sarcophagi. All this is but hypothesis. It is certain, however, that the maenadic alienation from the world of male order lived on in myth for a long time, and that we have here the representation of a mythical situation, definitely not a cult scene. Therefore, we cannot expect from this monument an exact analogy to the situation of the fleeing girl in the frieze of the mysteries.

Thus, the investigation has returned to its starting point, and the question—of what is the fleeing girl afraid?—remains unanswered. At this point it is best to look for the answers nearest at hand. If the reasons cited here for assigning the figure to the liknon scene are not valid, then we have to seek the reason for her fear in those groups that are closest to her.

Actually the fleeing girl finds herself in a situation which also could daunt others. She is clearly the only human being among the strange phantoms of mythology who, however, still seem to be so real. All the same, she pays attention neither to the singing Silenus nor to his neighbors, the unnatural shepherds. She looks back rather to the group with the mask which is next to her on the rear wall (Figs. 9, 13), like someone who runs away from the object of his fright but still cannot avert his eyes. Her gesture indicates fear mixed with surprise. Thus, there is every indication that the fleeing girl and the group with the mask form a whole with regard to content. On this point I agree with Matz, who not long ago discussed the group with the mask in detail.[36]

The painter of the frieze of the mysteries prefers a drawing style with definite outlines to the more impressionistic effects of contemporary colorists. As such he is a follower of Parrhasios rather than of Zeuxis. Like all draughtsmen he loves the difficult. The group with the mask is a brilliant example of his art. Three figures are arranged on three planes from the background directly toward the onlooker. At the very back a young satyr bends forward so that the mask which he holds up with his right hand appears above and even a little in front of the seated Silenus; the mask's beard slightly overlaps his furrowed forehead, which this time is wreathed with ivy. He himself holds a silver vessel with both hands, and the central figure, again a young fellow with pointed ears, bends so deeply into it that one perceives more of his head than of his face. The drinking vessel too is seen from underneath, foreshortened. Silenus, however, does not pay any attention to his action. His face is turned away, and his rolling eyes seem to follow the fleeing girl on the other side.

The group is conspicuous in its spatial compactness as well as in the acute frontality and the strong foreshortening which seems to include the onlooker in the event.[37] Actually, two actions are taking place simultaneously. A mask is being held up and exhibited as if it were a symbol with a meaning of its own. One must assume, however, that the youthful satyr has just taken the mask off Silenus. Thus, the unmasking equals an unveiling and corresponds to the unveiling of the phallus symbol on the other side of the group of gods. The arrangement of the pictorial parts on the rear wall is axial and symmetric also with regard to its content. The mask, while it strikes terror, still resembles the comparatively mild face of Silenus. I believe we know the name of the mask. It is Akratos, the daemon of the unmixed wine which, mysteriously murmuring, ferments in new casks until they are opened in the spring. The daemon too is alarming.[38] Thus, a reason supported by ancient sources is given here for the fear of the fleeing girl. It seems to me, therefore, that the best answer to the question of why the girl is behaving as she does is indicated by the monument itself, namely, that she is afraid of the daemonic mask and at the same time amazed by the double play, the two-faced nature of Silenus. Looking back she recognizes him, is frightened, and flees. It is possible or, rather, likely that this double play between mask and reality includes still other meanings which we have not yet discovered, but let us not speculate on them. In any case, here the viewer learns to know, guided by the wise Silenus, the second side of Dionysiac ecstasy: after the *enthusiasmos* of music, the magic of wine.

Another problem arises from the second action, the offering of the drinking vessel. Does it represent an oracular scene or simply the consumption of the offered drink?[39] The question is outside the immediate range of my investigation and cannot be decided by mere inspection. An oracle or prophecy from a reflection in the wine— just as in modern times from coffee grounds—was ancient practice. The evidence goes back to the early classical period.[40] But who can declare with certainty whether the young satyr gazes or drinks? A possibility must definitely be reserved for the latter. The vessel itself, a silver skyphos, resembles the traditional *akratophoron*.[41] But no matter what is happening here, wine is the main agent. While Silenus offers the cup, the mask hangs above him, like a sign board not to be overlooked. Is an invitation conveyed by the glance of his large eyes over toward the corner? Does a call come forth from his open lips? Does the girl withdraw from these?

THE FLAGELLATION (Figs. 10, 14)

The flagellation group, next to the liknon scene at the far right end of the rear wall and overlapping the adjoining corner of the southern side wall, represents the strangest episode of the entire frieze, the winged, striking woman is its most bizarre figure. Her bizarre character, however, is more make-believe than real. The ancient tradition from which she originated and to which she belongs can be clearly shown.

Various interesting attempts have been made to define her; therefore a detailed description of her strange appearance does not have to be repeated.[42] Obviously, she is a daemonic being, indeed a spirit of darkness equipped with large dark wings like the night.[43] She lifts a switch with her right hand, ready to strike. The upper part of her body is naked, and a short garment is draped around her hips but does not seem to be knotted. In addition, she wears high boots. Suggestions for naming the strange figure have been made, but all raise serious doubts. If one considers the objections all together, one recognizes what they have in common. The reconciliation of the obvious facts—the given representations and modern thoughts about them with ancient ideas about images and modes of thinking—has not yet been achieved.

Aidos also has to be ruled out here. One only has to realize that this personification would in Latin be called *Pudicitia* in order to see how unsuitable the costume would be for her representation. It is equally unnecessary to argue in detail whether this figure is either a winged Artemis or the constellation Virgo, since we can accept Matz's judicious comments regarding both suggestions.[44] It is more doubtful whether M. P. Nilsson's advice, not to look first for the name but rather for the function of the puzzling figure, will produce an answer.[45] This function—the blow she is about to strike—constitutes a problem; its special purpose might emerge only from knowledge of her name.

Nilsson and Matz have, however, indicated the method which promises a solution to the problem. The striking figure is certainly a daemon, not a goddess. At the time the frieze of the mysteries was probably produced, the second quarter of the first century B.C., such figures of daemons had long been a part of art in Italy. Late Etruscan monuments, especially funerary urns, show them in an abundance of variations (Fig. 15), and some of those examples come quite close to the winged figure in dress as well as conduct.[46] But these Etruscan pictorial fantasies themselves go back to the early beginnings of Greek art in South Italy, namely, to the wealth of images on painted Apulian and Tarentine vases. The Artemis-like costume, the wings, and

Fig. 11. Phallus and fleeing winged woman, Campana relief, Paris, Louvre

Fig. 12. Phallus in the liknon and dancing maenad, mosaic from Roman villa near Djemila, Algeria

Fig. 13. Frieze, detail, Fig. 1 (V)

Fig. 14. Frieze, detail, Fig. 1 (VIII)

Fig. 15. Etruscan urn from Volterra with winged female daemon, Rome, Musei Vaticani

Fig. 16. Red-figured calyx-krater from Ruvo with punishment of Lykurgos, London, British Museum

Fig. 17. Roman oscillum with Bacchic ritual, Boston, Museum of Fine Arts

the weird, often underworldly, meaning are already found together there. It is important that these dark beings sometimes have their names inscribed on the vases, or that they appear in mythical contexts from which the intended name can be deduced with great likelihood, even if the inscribed name is missing. Dike and Nemesis, whose names have recently been introduced into the discussion about the winged figure on the frieze, belong on this list.[47] Among the female daemons of this Graeco-Italic pictorial world is one whose character seems to me eminently well suited for the activity of the winged figure on the frieze and for the context in which she appears. I am speaking of the daemon Lyssa.

This figure is properly a psychological personification, first in myth and then especially in Euripidean drama. Madness and indomitable passions are her doing. One might say that she represents this madness in person, and consequently at the same time its incomprehensible and therefore daemonic origin. Beyond this general description, she has been accepted, at least since Euripides, as a Dionysiac daemon. She arouses Dionysiac madness, the whirling passion of maenads or the blinding frenzy with which the god of wine strikes his victims. Therefore, her picture appears in illustrations of such events as, for instance, the Lykurgos myth (Fig. 16).[48] The means she uses are a blow or sting, a *kentron* or whip. She goads or whips up passions, just as the modern metaphor puts it. Thus, she does exactly what the winged figure on the frieze, shown in an attire that still resembles the named, older representations, sets out to do. The conceptual and iconographical concordances are so close that I do not hesitate to use the name Lyssa for this figure as well. No other personification or daemon we know matches so closely the lashing, winged figure of the frieze, and none is so much at home in the world of the Bacchic imagination. Thus, we might conclude that Lyssa is at work here too. The blow she is ready to strike—she herself in a swift, almost dancing pose—is aimed at the half-naked girl who kneels next to her at the beginning of the south long wall.

THE MAENADS (Figs. 10, 14)

The stance which the painter has given his winged figure is indeed noteworthy. The torsion of the upper half of the body is certainly grounded on the powerful swinging of the right arm and is a strong emotional action. The position of the legs, however, is quite unusual for somebody who deals a blow. The impression is that of a volatile apparition barely touching the ground. Half floating, her wings seem to carry her more than her feet, and her left leg, which is put forward on account of the quick turn, almost completely covers the other one, resulting in quite an unstable position indeed. It will hardly make the lashing more effective. This but transitory step, demanding continuous movement, looks like the pose of a dancer. The naked dancer on the other side of the flagellation group performs almost the same step, seen from the back, in accordance with a known Neo-Attic schema.[49] Thus, Lyssa herself is introduced as a maenadic character. While she whips, she imparts her nature to her victim.

Until now, no mention has been made of maenads in the frieze. This too is a strange situation because in the more conventional Dionysiac representations maenads and satyrs usually appear in great numbers. The maenads' dance is ecstatic but at the same time it is believed to have a relieving and calming effect.[50] We know that in the interpretation of basic facts, the emphasis can vary—in the Dionysiac as well as in every other religion. Perhaps the trend we are dealing with here can be explained sometime in the future but first of all the fundamental facts have to be established. From the above observations, however, the following seems to be clear. The blow dealt by the winged person cannot be interpreted as punishment or judgment. Its meaning might be an initiation or a transformation of a natural human being into the spiritual state of a maenad. Thereby the still missing third Dionysiac mystery, ecstacy through dance, would have been attained.

This explanation implies that the four women at the southeast corner are natural, not mythical characters. This was never doubted with respect to the two dressed figures, as well as to the one kneeling who rests her head on the lap of the fully dressed, seated woman. But then the dancing girl who is shown from the back cannot be meant, in this context, as a mythical figure, since the four figures together form one of those closed groups so characteristic for the style of the frieze. Also with regard to content, the dancer cannot be excluded from this union. It is noteworthy that the world of the daemons affects the human world visibly and directly in this part of the frieze; the flagellation group is an exception in this respect. It is indeed the very task of Lyssa to excite in natural otherwise normal people the kind of passion which alienates a human being from himself. This was exactly her role in Greek drama and Apulian vase paintings.[51] She herself is a conceptional abstraction, her beating or whipping is to be understood allegorically, not as reality, for actually she strikes a blow at the mind not at the body.

It is not so easy to discover the additional relations and actions which unite the four women who are placed as a group opposite the striking figure. The kneeling girl seems to expect the impending blow in this position. She is almost naked, her only garment is a purple cloak which reveals her as it loosely slips away; her long hair is untied and hangs dishevelled around her face, as if she had already become a maenad. It is significant that her eye is almost closed. This could mean sleep, although her posture does not correspond with that of sleeping persons who are commonly represented in ancient art with one hand over their head. Sleep, dream, and happy wakening often seem to have meant more than what is obvious for the female companions of Dionysus, for whom the sleeping Ariadne was the prototype. Maenads lapse into the insensible sleep of exhaustion, and rites, the meaning of which is unknown to us, are performed over sleeping, maenad-like women (Fig. 17).[52] Dreams in which the sleeper sees a supernatural winged creature occur even outside the Dionysiac sphere, as on Roman coins which have so successfully been interpreted by A. Alföldi as representing Sulla's dream.[53] Incidentally, this representation also points out that the dream appearance of a winged being, perhaps even of one who strikes a blow, cannot have been as exceptional to the ancient viewer as to the modern. However, yet another consideration is pertinent where Bacchic scenes are represented. One should recall here that the condition of the sleeper might hold, among other things, a reference to the word μυεῖν, with the meaning "to close one's eyes." Therefore, it appears possible to explain the nearly closed eye of the kneeling girl in the frieze of the Villa of the Mysteries in the same way, that is to say, as the condition of the initiate who shuts his eyes.[54] Dream and sleep can thus paraphrase the experience of the person who is to be initiated, just as the veiling of the head seems to fulfill the same condition in representations of other rites.[55] In all these pictorial and ritual metaphors which are used so often in Bacchic iconography, the idea of "not seeing" can be recognized. The pictorial invention of the kneeling girl and her protectress is so far unique, but the sleep-like condition so strangely rendered here establishes sufficiently a connection with other pictures and customs of mysteries, so that it might be assumed that the whole scene actually represents an event concerning mysteries. The lashing daemon then turns out to be an allegory, indispensable for our understanding. However, the separation of symbol and reality cannot be carried out in every detail in this part of the frieze since the event shown, even if it can be regarded as a real ritual, was most likely itself of a symbolic nature.

The seated woman in this ritual can obviously be called a helper and is probably a friendly character. But she will not ward off the blow. On the contrary, while she looks up at the already present (or awaited?) daemon, she holds the young girl's head on her knees with her left hand and with her right clears her back, so it seems, of the long tresses. Her part is to instruct and to prepare, for she evidently knows what has to happen. Her dress looks elegant. Around her knees she wears a white cloak, beautifully painted, and underneath, a thin chiton which has slipped down from her right shoulder over the arm. The painter has generally made a point, in this group, of delineating all clothing as loosely tied, not closely knotted. Thus, the hair of the kneeling girl is also let down, not bound. Are we to recognize the liberating power of Liber in the freely falling costumes? Another acolyte, approaching from the right, fully dressed in a purple garment, brings the thyrsos. Is it her own or is it to be handed over to the kneeling girl as the badge of honor for a maenad? The dancer in the foreground, with her arms uplifted and her hands holding *crotala*, is, however, certainly a maenad figure. Her only garment is a narrow, gold-colored veil which flutters from her shoulder. And yet her dance is strikingly quiet, we could almost call it formal. The Bacchic ecstasy here lacks all wildness. It seems to be more trance than frenzy.

We are confronted here with another problem that has been repeatedly discussed in the past. Are we to regard the frieze as a continuous whole, a sequence of interrelated actions, or, on the contrary, as a paratactic series of unconnected Dionysiac and ritual recollections indifferent to each other in their meaning? R. Herbig has pleaded emphatically for the second alternative.[56] Even so, I do not believe that the question has been settled. The argument against a modern, naturalistic interpretation has to be considered, even though any such attempt will prove to be unworkable since the typically Roman, centralized arrangement of the frieze brings it to naught. Its accentuated center, the group of the gods, interrupts any natural chronological order of the events which we might assume to exist. Neither are there any portrait likenesses which, for instance, might enable us to recognize the same person in different situations.[57] Even Silenus, who certainly occurs twice, appears in each case with a different physiognomy. But all this does not imply that no meaning at all can be found in the sequence of the episodes. There still remains the possibility that the entering young woman, the fleeing girl, and the initiate of the flagellation group stand for the same person in the proper sense of a continuous representation, or that the same three figures depict three different stages of a consistent action in a continuous story. Both solutions are possible. But then we also have to ask whether the kneeling girl and the naked dancer in the flagellation group are two different persons or whether, in the manner of Roman "continuous narration," they rather depict the same person twice, in different moments of a coherent event which follow hard upon each other. It might be difficult to prove that either of the two alternatives is correct, yet it appears to me that the second is not less likely than the first. Assuming this to be true, the situation represented could possibly be translated into words in the following way. The initiate expects Lyssa's blow; once struck she is transformed. She is now *the* maenad. Otherwise one would have to say that she is merely one of the maenads belonging to the throng.

THE BRIDAL SCENES (Figs. 18–20)

The large window on the south wall is next to the group with the maenad. Beyond the window the bridal scenes begin. They continue past the southwest corner to the wide door on the west wall and on its other side to the corner of the north wall. The so-called *Domina* occupies the narrow space between the west door and the northwest corner (Fig. 20). With her the frieze comes to an end. This follows from the fact that, among other things, only at this corner does the depicted action not continue on to the adjacent wall.[58] The north wall begins with the already mentioned door, now serving as an entrance, which leads to the adjoining bedroom. On the other side of this door is the veiled woman whom we can identify as the first figure of the frieze on account of the entire arrangement of this corner. Turning her back on the *Domina* she starts on her way to the rear wall, where the group of the gods is located. The *Domina,* in turn, directs her glance toward the near end of the opposite south wall. She does not pay any attention at all to the veiled figure on the other side and does not even seem to be aware of her presence. The lack of contact between these two corner figures not only points out the beginning and the end of the frieze but also the direction we have to follow in "reading" it.

By describing the last pictures of the frieze as bridal scenes, this investigation returns to the basic observations which Bieber made years ago. An essentially different interpretation is hardly possible. The bridal scenes represent a closed sequence that consists of two related pictures: the dressing of the bride (Fig. 18), and the waiting bride on the *kline* (Fig. 20). Both themes derive from an old pictorial tradition which originated in classical art.[59] It is unnecessary to enter here into the long history of marriage pictures. Their popularity began to decrease only during the Roman empire

Fig. 18. Frieze, detail, Fig. 1 (IX)

Fig. 19. Frieze, detail, Fig. 1 (X)

Fig. 20. Frieze, detail, Fig. 1 (IX)

Fig. 21. Aldobrandini Wedding, Rome, Musei Vaticani

Fig. 22. Frieze, detail, Fig. 1 (VI)

though in Roman-Campanian painting they were still considered essential. Consequently we must remember that at the time when the frieze was painted both themes belonged to an iconography of wedding scenes which had been traditional for some time. The selection of the themes proper, that is, of the situations represented, was Greek. The preparatory nature of the two moments likewise recalls their Greek origin; the actual wedding is not represented but only the preceding dressing of the bride and her waiting. On the other hand, we find Roman elements in details, especially in the underlying conceptions of customs and costume.

Among these details belongs, for example, the bride's coiffure, if, as I assume, Bieber's suggestion is correct. In the dressing scene her hair is being separated into strands. This corresponds with the manner of arranging from six different strands the complicated coiffure which the ritual of a Roman wedding, *confarreatio*, prescribed.[60] The symbolic details of this scene still await explanation. The hairdresser, whose task is obvious, is assisted by two half-grown, winged Erotes (Figs. 18, 19), the presence of whom in women's rooms stems from a Greek tradition, as do their occupations. Numerous examples are known. Even if the combination of such typical elements in the frieze of the mysteries did not amount to more than an embellished genre scene, it would still be one with symbolic undertones. The little Eros on the left holds up to the bride a mirror which does not have its usual round form but is, strangely enough, rectangular. Nevertheless, its purpose cannot be doubted: it shows a reflection. Behind the bride on the west wall stands the other winged little boy. Leaning his right arm on a pillar, he lifts his face and supports it with his right hand. With rapt attention he watches the dressing scene round the corner in front of him. His pose and mood belong to Pothos who represents the intense longing for love.[61] The mirror and his glance, both directed toward the same object, complement each other and the impression is one of a charade being acted out. However, this is not the place to attempt its interpretation.[62]

Concerning the details of the next picture, the waiting bride (Fig. 20), Herbig's last observations have the greatest importance. The furniture on which she is sitting is only partially shown for want of space. It is carefully rendered in a design which is clear but not in perspective; it cannot possibly be interpreted as an armchair. The furniture is without doubt a *kline* on high feet, which here can signify only the bridal bed.[63] The noble lady who presents herself to us as its owner rests her hand on the head of the bed. A comparison with the so-called Aldobrandini Wedding, which depicts a similar situation, might be interesting (Fig. 21) for there too the bride is waiting on her *kline*, but she is dressed in white and is more heavily veiled.[64] The face of the *Domina* is uncovered, the veil falls backward. She too looks thoughtful but her cloak is luxurious and colorful, the ring on her hand is visible, and the *tabellae*, the marriage contract, lie next to her.[65] It seems to me as though the Roman version of the old pictorial schema tends to bring to light the girl's new rank more than her hesitation. The *Domina* of the frieze of the mysteries is identified, above all, as a member of a social class with special obligations and privileges. Her festive clothing, the *praetexta* garments which are her new possession, demonstrates this. She has already risen to that peculiarly Roman privileged level of feminine society at which she will spend the rest of her life. That is to say, legally she is no longer considered as *vigro* but as *matrona*.

THE FRIEZE AS A WHOLE

All this has little to do with Bacchic rites and ideas. The connection between the bridal pictures and the other episodes of the frieze is not immediately clear, at least not for the modern, uninitiated viewer. We are definitely confronted with a problem which has so far defied all efforts made to solve it, but that is not reason enough to deny altogether that the bridal scenes belong to the frieze in content as well as in composition.[66] There is no authentic evidence in the painting itself to indicate a separation into two independent parts—unless one wants to interpret the interruptions which the room's architecture imposed on the painter as a mode of division. But in that case the dressing scene would have to be separated from the picture of the waiting bride and that would be most unlikely. The opposite assumption of an inner harmony of the whole frieze holds a greater probability. The argument can be strengthened by considering this harmony as a continuous narration, such as we have described it here. The dressing scene follows the maenad group and can be understood, in a certain sense, as its logical sequence. The progressive undressing of the main figure in the preceding groups is then completed with the naked dancer in the maenad group. The new investiture can now take place as a further step to a new level of meaning. The dancing girl actually looks toward the next scene, that is, away from her present surroundings. This play of glances points to continuity; thus, the maenad group no longer qualifies as the end of a composition. Very little more than what the painting itself intimates is known about the special "theology of dress" which might be preserved in the progressive changes and transformations of the costume.[67]

Thus, the main problem of the entire frieze is still hidden behind all the questions concerning details. How can the various pictures of the frieze of the mysteries be associated as an easily understood whole? In what way do the bridal scenes, for instance, belong to the Bacchic occurrences which above all give the frieze its characteristic quality? This last question, in my opinion, has not yet been answered in a satisfactory manner, and I doubt that the time for it has come. Dionysus was not originally an appropriate patron or model for the matrimonial institution.[68] There are, however, relatively early references to wedding pictures, perhaps used only as metaphors, which occur at least since classical times in the Dionysiac iconography,[69] but their relation to the actual social conditions of the time, that is, to real weddings, so far remains obscure. The so-called wedding of Dionysus and the Basilinna was a single Athenian cult episode.[70] Dionysiac consecrations, if they occurred at all in the fifth century B.C., normally promised everything else but matrimonial order, as we know from Euripides. Moreover, ancient weddings were virtually civil acts, not consecrations. How does all this fit together? The corpus of Dionysiac sarcophagi promises to add new material to these questions. We shall have to wait for it.[71]

It will be helpful to make at least a preliminary resumé of the above observations. Two conclusions immediately emerge in retrospect. The first one is a matter of a simple statistical fact. If we consider again the difference established at the beginning between real and fictitious characters among the persons in the frieze, we arrive at a clear and important result. The figures who recognizably represent real persons are all women. Not a single male can be found among them, as a matter of fact, with the exception of the reading boy. All the male figures of the frieze, the sileni as well as the satyrs, represent fictitious characters. All those who carry out cult acts are real persons, always women, with the exception again of the boy whose reading is being supervised by a woman. The observation confirms the generally accepted opinion that the scenes depicted allude to actual rites and to the ideas and mythical narratives present in them. Moreover, it leads to the conclusion that the represented actions must be attributed to a women's cult, that means a cult which was exclusively performed by women and which most likely, was only accessible to women. So far as the monument, as the only evidence, justifies an opinion, it must be assumed that no male participants were tolerated in these religious exercises.

A second conclusion concerns the obvious lack of consistency in the meaning of the represented situations. An analysis in this respect shows that we are dealing with three parts. Their diversity is expressed also in the entire arrangement of the frieze. Actions prescribed by the cult form the first part. Neither mythical nor allegorical elements interfere with their reality, which must be interpreted literally. It might be difficult for just this reason to recognize the specific meaning of these actions. Perhaps they are Dionysiac in character, but there is no need to explain them on that basis, even though it remains likely that a mystery rite is being performed. The unmistakably Dionysiac part of the frieze starts only with the singing Silenus and extends without interruption to the dancing maenad. Next come the bridal scenes, the third part of the composition. Here again, Dionysiac allusions cannot be detected. As so often on Roman monuments, the arrangement then is clearly in three parts. The Dionysiac part occupies a cardinal place since it not only covers the entire rear wall but spreads, as with two outstretched arms, to the adjoining long walls, requiring approximately an additional third of each. From all this, we may infer therefore that the cult and the rites demonstrated by the frieze were originally not homogeneous. They were not all Dionysiac in the same way.

THE GROUP OF THE GODS (Figs. 9, 22)

From a formal as well as a thematic analysis of the frieze it becomes apparent that the east short wall is its principal part. Here, between the group with the mask and the unveiling of the liknon we find Dionysus himself, the *deus praesens*, united with Ariadne in mutual embrace. This group too deserves critical comment, but, unfortunately, it can only be briefly indicated here. The destruction of the upper part of the representation is a great loss for us, for the group is beautifully painted and differs considerably from the rest of the frieze not only in the size of the figures but also in style. To start with the content, Dionysus sits on a slightly lower bench next to Ariadne. The preserved remains of the painting suggest that she was a powerful figure, matron-like in appearance rather than maidenly. Leaning decidedly backward, Dionysus clasps her with both his arms while she holds him in hers. With his left arm on Ariadne's thigh, he reposes in her lap. The situation which we have thus described is meaningful in several respects, for among other things it can be understood as a thematic, though not a formal, parallel to the kneeling girl who under quite different circumstances buries her head in the lap of her protectress. A prototypical relationship is indicated here; it should not be overlooked even though it cannot be fully explained.

But the ecstasy is over within the group of the gods, and a state of tranquillity has been reached. With the unused thyrsos beside him, Dionysus has slipped back to repose. The shoe, dropped carelessly, seems conspicuous to the onlooker, but it does not necessarily signify more than an accompanying detail, a mute and eloquent testimony to the calm after the storm.[72] Dionysus looks up to Ariadne and although we cannot tell any more whether she returned the amorous glance, it is most likely she did. The group's *ethos*—to use the ancient technical term—was clearly romantic, concentrated on "finally having found each other," the transport of love with a happy ending. Once more one comes across a parallel rich in associations. This time it is the exchange of glances between Dionysus and the exalted bride which is echoed by the gods of love in the dressing scene. The god, so it seems, is connected with those who belong to him in many ways, by experience and by fate.

Other peculiarities of this representation belong to the compositional structure of the work, though they should remain part of the question of content as well. Actually, it is wrong to talk about a group of gods here since Ariadne is, strictly speaking, no deity. Only Dionysus is a god. Nevertheless, the group has been placed in the frieze facing the beholder like a cult image. It comes forward out of the background in a frontal-rectangular way like the nearby group with the mask, but not as abruptly. The diagonal position of Dionysus reveals the Hellenistic origin of the formal invention. It has often been pointed out—and with justification—that the fact that Ariadne occupies a higher place constitutes an anomaly.[73] Moreover, the middle axis of the wall, or rather of the entire room, coincides almost exactly with the middle axis of the enthroned Ariadne. Thus, she is in every way the central figure and therefore the main deity of the frieze. Dionysus rests by her side, looking up to her. This group resembles (not without reason) Ariosto's much admired pair of lovers, Rinaldo resting in Armida's lap. The exchange of glances has been described by Ariosto in the same manner. He even used the metaphor of the eye as the mirror of the beloved, which perhaps already underlies the exchange of glances of the gods of love in the dressing scene.[74] There is every indication then that the group of gods in the frieze of the mysteries represents a very special and independent variation of the Dionysus myth, in fact a new interpretation of the myth with the roles of the participants reversed. The god has become the *paredros* of the beloved whom he exalted and she is the reigning goddess. As Curtius has already seen, the idea was probably not Greek, but it does belong to the world of Hellenized mother goddesses in Asia

Minor.[75] We now understand that the women dedicated to this cult over which the mythical couple presided cannot have been indifferent to the new and unusual interpretation of the mythical pair, an interpretation which differed so widely from that of classical antiquity.

THE CULT: A CONJECTURE

The group of Dionysus and Ariadne was not an unknown work, and is the only part of the frieze to which we have unmistakable reminiscenses in other, very different kinds of monuments. A cameo in the Kunsthistorisches Museum in Vienna, as well as a Domitianic coin of the city of Smyrna, render the same group.[76] It is most unlikely that even a single one of these rather summary repetitions goes back to the Pompeian painting. As so often happens in Roman art, we are dealing with reproductions of an older *opus nobile*, and the group on the frieze can be only a link in the same chain of replicas. Thus, in all probability, it is itself a copy after a Hellenistic painting, the original of which would have to be placed in the late fourth or early third century B.C. Evidently it was a work of high quality, an unusually brilliant and impressive invention. Chances are that the Dionysiac couple was its only subject with no other persons or narrative content being present. The copy would not have been included in the frieze without thought, but nevertheless it is like a foreign insertion, a quotation. I do not assume that the rest of the figures in the frieze were copies, but if it were so their prototypes would have to be sought elsewhere and above all in a much later stylistic period.

An attempt to make a further statement about this lost original would be sheer hypothesis. If, nevertheless, this essay closes with such a conjecture, it does so only because the ancient tradition offers a reference of great interest for the problems under discussion. The catalogues of Pliny in fact contain a title which is immediately conclusive for the group of the frieze of the mysteries, and thus for the probable prototype as well. The picture in question, representing Dionysus and Ariadne, is by Aristeides of Thebes, an early Hellenistic painter whose work could be seen in the motherland and in Asia Minor.[77] The couple could have been portrayed in various ways, and nothing states that the group by Aristeides looked exactly like the one we are seeking. Pliny, however, mentions an additional fact. Aristeides' painting "formerly" was to be seen in the temple of Ceres in Rome. 'Formerly" probably refers to the fire of the year 31 B.C. which badly damaged the temple. The painting might have been destroyed or else it was taken to another place.[78] In any event, it is interesting that a famous painting with this title was in the temple of Ceres in Rome just at the same time when the Pompeian frieze was painted.

The temple of Ceres at the foot of the Aventine, probably under today's Bocca della Verita, was a very ancient and special place. The history of its foundation connects it with the revolution which established the Roman republic. On the advice of the Sibylline Books, the cult was regulated in 493 B.C. according to the Campanian pattern. From this time dates the official name, the temple of Ceres, Liber, and

Libera. Since Dionysus and Ariadne could be meant by the last two names—at least since Hellenistic times—Aristeides' picture was indeed in the right place.[79]

In spite of the relatively rich sources for its history, our idea of the religion which the temple represented is not as clear as one would wish.[80] Ceres, like the Greek Demeter, was by her nature a goddess of women. Grain, seed, and harvest, the fruits of the fields, were her concern. An assimilation with Demeter suggested itself and was carried out early; and with Demeter came her Greek mythology, the legend of the kidnapped daughter, and possibly also a new ritual. In the early first century B.C., the period which concerns us here, the connection with Campania is well attested. Even some of the temple's personnel were called from there.[81] But that does not mean that the cult did not maintain a certain local character, for the temple of Ceres had been declared a sanctuary of the plebs and thus served a segment of the population classified as such only in Rome. The part taken by the town's matrons at the temple's calendar feasts was based on similar social principles and likewise had a local characteristic, a Roman feature.

Women's cults existed in Greece too, especially in the service of Demeter. The Attic Thesmophorai are an obvious example.[82] Nowhere, however, were these institutions so frequent as in Rome. Their membership was firmly organized there in a corporate manner, the basis for which is found not only in the Etruscan-Roman family structure, which granted a relatively large measure of authority to married women, at least inside their home, but also in the sacral order of the state, which could not spare any of its members for multiple tasks. The ruling women of the great families, patrician as well as plebeian in origin, formed in this sacral range a social class with privileges and obligations inside and outside the home. It was for the common interest that these obligations were met regularly. The performance itself lay in the hands of authorized women.[83]

A short survey of these conditions at the end of the Republican period yields two peculiar results. The majority of those cults which were regularly practiced by the matrons are addressed to ancient native deities, often of an obscure significance but endowed with functions proper to the female sphere of influence, such as the Fortunae, Mater Matuta, Bona Dea.[84] In this sphere Ceres is the object of a cult having more than Roman-Latin standing. Secondly, all these cults share a high degree of social exclusiveness. The positions, as well as access to them, are limited, even if in different ways. The matrons themselves are recruited from the leading class of society. The exclusion of men is even more significant, especially in the secret rituals of Bona Dea and in the temple of Ceres. Here then a principle which was to protect an easily vulnerable ritual comes into being, a principle that the maenads of Dionysus had enacted only in a mythical form. The women entrusted with this ritual meet as a closed society. During the ceremony which lasts one night, they are suspended from the institutions of male society. The office they were charged with did not even tolerate male presence.

CERES, LIBER, AND LIBERA

The following questions concerning the great frieze in the Villa of the Mysteries arise from the circumstances just mentioned. According to common iconography, the frieze definitely does not represent a mythical bacchanal, and whether or not it follows any coherent iconography at all remains uncertain. As we stated above, the frieze consists of three sections, the first of which represents cult scenes to be viewed as real. The main part contains mythical detail and, in addition, such symbolic acts like the flagellation scene as can expound the opinions and expectations of a real cult group. Real persons, for instance, the fleeing girl, participate in these episodes. Whether the acts themselves should be judged as actual happenings must remain to be seen. It is at least doubtful whether the kneeling victim of the flagellation really received a blow from the hand of a human being whose place in the painting is taken by the winged daemon. One might ask as well whether the nakedness of the dancing girl is to be understood as real—which would be possible—or only as a symbolic attribute belonging to the world of maenads. Nevertheless, it is certain that the main part of the frieze deals with Dionysiac ideas. Into these Dionysiac elements, mythical or symbolic, a cult scene, the unveiling of the phallus in the liknon, has been inserted, the reality of which we have no reason to doubt. Thus, in the main part of the frieze we are dealing with a mixed iconography which contains fictitious as well as real images, traditional as well as iconographically unusual ones. The third part, however, with the dressing of the bride and the bride waiting on the bridal bed, follows a consistent and traditional iconography of wedding scenes with some realistic additions and alterations taking into consideration specifically Roman views. On the whole, the iconography of the frieze shows a conspicuous lack of homogeneity. This fact supports the assumption that the frieze was created for a special purpose or for the purpose of a special cult community. It is rich in original inventions.

For the reason just mentioned, it is worthwhile to pursue the allusion to a possible connection with the cult in the Roman temple of Ceres. At least the reference indicates an area of historical reality where a cult group like the proposed sodality of the frieze could find a place among existing institutions, that is to say, among the women's cults of the Roman matrons. Not many of the known Roman city cults can be considered for our question as not all of them were suitable for export. Outside Rome the Italic Bacchanalia ought to be given attention first, Campania having been one of their original provinces. In the beginning, they too were esoteric women's cults, but their exclusiveness was no longer maintained after the senatorial edict of 186 B.C.[86] Possibly the frieze includes reminiscences of several of their original observances, but as a whole, the frieze refers to something else and its secret lies in its very lack of homogeneity.

For this reason I shall return once more to the assumption that there is a connection between the frieze of the mysteries and the cult in the Roman temple of Ceres. The cult was most fashionable.The fact that many *Augustae* attached great importance to being portrayed as priestesses of Ceres can be partly explained by the social prestige of her Roman temple. Although it was generally referred to as the temple of Ceres, we must not forget that the goddess shared this place of worship with two equally famous partners. The painting by Aristeides, which Pliny mentioned and which might have been copied in the frieze of the mysteries, reminds us of this fact. It is difficult to imagine how this partnership affected the practical cult since the temple's calendar feasts all refer to the name of Ceres. This does not mean that the other partners were neglected; rather, several cults were superimposed upon each other, a phenomenon which must have occurred at a much earlier time. In classical Greece too Demeter was sometimes associated with Dionysus, and a unification of the cults of Dionysus and the queen of the underworld, Kore-Persephone, probably took place in Greek South Italy.[87] Old religions, however, do not cancel each other out, nor do they really merge, but one of them could be superimposed on another. In this process the original ideas, sentiments, and symbols are maintained though new legends spring from them. Ceres was and remained the autonomous force of the fields and the mother permanently fertile yet in need of fecundation, as the soil is in need of rain. The male turns here into a symbol, since a personality is not required. But the fruit, the corn, the mother's daughter, is personified. When a man intercedes as a third party, he becomes a robber. He is also a symbol, but this time simultaneously of death and authority, like Hades. The myth of Dionysus is not applicable to this situation because the wine god is altogether personal; he is master in his own realm, a liberator and a redeemer. Yet in a cult triad such as the one of the temple of Ceres, superimpositions of this kind, with an uncertain result, have to be expected. Ceres was an ancient Italic goddess. Perhaps even the myth of the daughter was already a Greek addition. Dionysus certainly came later and with him Libera-Ariadne, his companion. The question as to how the contradictions—if indeed they were perceived as such—were cleared up is beyond the scope of this essay. Here we must remember only that they existed.[88]

The ancient sources about the cults of the temple of Ceres are rather scarce, but they report extraordinarily interesting details. The calendar of feasts listed three main holidays, one of them a yearly mystery ritual, the *sacrum anniversarium Cereris*. This was a nocturnal ceremony after the Greek pattern, a παννυχίς: *pervigilia Cereris*. Its date has not been transmitted precisely, but it may have been a movable feast; a date in midsummer around harvest time is likely.[89] It was certainly a secret rite executed by women. Men were denied access. A similarly transmitted and perhaps mimetic act concerning the rape of Kore, the *Orci nuptiae*, is generally associated with this mystery, but not for good reason in spite of the fact that the recovery of the raped daughter, played a part, though not necessarily in the form of a performance of a cult drama. Even if such a performance belonged to the rites of the *pervigilium*, it would not have required the entire night. There must have been enough time for other celebrations which are now unknown to us. These could have easily included additional and more clandestine thesmophoric ceremonies.[90]

That the nocturnal ceremony in the temple of Ceres included special meanings is clear from the known taboos established for that night. The membership is of importance: women only, and among them *matronae* as well as *virgines*. The words *pater* and *filia* were forbidden. While the latter prohibition might be interpreted as a gesture of respect for the bereaved mother, the former cannot be explained by the same argument.[91] In the corn sanctuary, the sacred center of the Roman plebs, the patrician title was probably not very highly regarded. Besides, *pater* was also a sacral title. *Dispater* could displease Ceres likewise and could be even more offensive than the word *filia*. Moreover, Liber Pater must have been affected by the sacral prohibition, even though he was a partner in the cult. Whatever the reasons, the effect of the taboos remained the same and was not accidental. We could call it a verbal supplement to the ritual exclusion of men, that is, the ritual denial of paternal power in the family of women for the duration of one night.

In addition, there are two more prohibitions. The word "wine" was not to be pronounced. A similar prohibition prevailed in the nocturnal ceremony of the Bona Dea which is comparable in some respects.[92] But in the temple of Ceres, Liber, and Libera, this taboo is even more conspicuous. We cannot escape the assumption that it also was directed against Liber Pater, the co-partner whose power is restricted for the duration of the mystery in still another way—by simply not being mentioned. Secondly, before the start of the ceremony, the members had to observe a period of sexual continence which lasted at least nine hours and more likely, nine days. This too probably can be viewed as a thesmophoric arrangement.[93]

The conflicting aims within a merged cult dedicated to an official triad of gods can be of special interest here. They are the noticeable scars left by a superimposition of cults or by an early syncretism.[94] The contradictions can undoubtedly shed light on the comparable inconsistency of the iconography as well as of the content in the large frieze in the Villa of the Mysteries at Pompeii. The frieze itself forms a triad, a kind of colossal triptych, as we stated above. Here too tensions appear between the members of the triad, although the three parts that constitute the frieze cannot be named as accurately as the triad of the temple of Ceres. Therefore, it is not plausible that the frieze describes the cult of the temple of Ceres or any other existing cult, since the numerous symbolic additions speak against it. Nevertheless, there are significant similarities between the ritual of the Roman Ceres performed by the matrons and the women's cult in the frieze of the mysteries.

To begin with the dissimilarities, the main part of the Pompeian frieze is clearly a Bacchic representation, perhaps even an illustration of a Bacchic mystery. Music, wine, and dance are its three mystical aspects. That the group of gods, which perhaps could be seen in the temple of Ceres as well, hints at something else, was recognized long ago. The oneness of love is split into a duality in which the god does not hold the highest position. The goddess occupies a higher throne. Thus, the ruling deity is, at least in this place, a woman. In this lies the cause of a tension which, in a similar way, has also arisen in the triad of the temple of Ceres. This tension is superhuman; its place is in the realm of the gods.

From now on the similarities become more distinct. By their very nature, symbolic works of art such as the frieze neither illustrate principles nor express dogmas. They inspire thought. We have to consider for instance that two important cult symbols in the frieze are not accepted. The girl flees from Akratos. Then Lyssa, about to administer the blow which will stir the maenad to her own unique passion, turns away from the unveiling of the phallus, in defense, as it were. It looks as if she wanted to say, not now, not here. With that she holds her hand up defensively, almost in the same way as the dancing maenad does on the mosaic from Djemila (Fig. 12).[95] A parallel exists in the nocturnal ceremony of Ceres where the women are not allowed to pronounce the word "wine" and where sexual continence before the ceremony—hence rejection of the male—is strictly required. Enough reason has been given to acknowledge significant agreements even though the rite and the painting call for different interpretations. We may not claim complete certainty, but the religious conditions of both lines of behavior, as well as ancient reports, support the likely conclusion that in the two cases the underlying purpose of the cult was the same. Even if the other members of the triad, Liber and Libera, were not mentioned in the mystery of Ceres in Rome and only Bacchus and Ariadne were visible on the frieze in Pompeii, the rites, whether depicted or as in Rome only performed, had a similar effect. Both produced in a symbolic way the detachment of the participating women from the patriarchal family unit. In the mystery of Ceres this is accomplished by the ritual independence of the matrons and in the retinue of Bacchus by the maenad who evades marriage as a result of a mystic initiation. The deities otherwise so contrary, Ceres and the god of wine, are on this point of one mind, or nearly so.

It follows that in both women's cults, the Campanian as well as the Roman, the Dionysiac religion underwent a speculative interpretation different from the traditional Bacchic visions of paradise which are so common in art. This interpretation, however, was not entirely new. On the contrary, a good deal of that primal temperament which once animated the even wilder Dionysiac testimonies of classical times was preserved in its Roman-Italic guise. The known relations between Campania and the Roman cult of Ceres, Liber, and Libera help make the typological concurrences of the content historically plausible.[96]

Our attempt at explanation must halt here, at least for the time being, for many details are still missing. The statue of the empress Livia stood in the garden of the villa. Was there a relationship between her likeness, which after all could not be found in every garden in Pompeii, and the esoteric women's club which perhaps still met there during her lifetime?[97] And on a much lower level, one finds on the walls of the same villa the exasperated epigram of a frustrated lover, Ceres mea, which M. Della Corte has published with such perception.[98] Is all this mere accident? The bridal scenes especially have not yet been properly placed in the structure of the whole. A final remark should therefore be added in regard to this last question which has always been one of the main problems of the frieze.

The answer to the question is not made easier by the analysis expounded here. In it the world of maenads and of the family appear as separate institutions. Even the transformation into a maenad as it is represented in the frieze has an institutional meaning in that the new member of the society of initiates is furnished with the thyrsos, invested, so to speak.[99] There seem to be only contrasts between the maenad and the declared bride. No link exists. They belong to separate worlds and transitions are unthinkable.

Nevertheless, not transitions but parallels between these antagonistic characters become visible in the same analysis. Both represent social lines of conduct, effected by rites in the case of the maenad, sanctioned by rites in the case of the bride. The bride too submits to ceremonies, although not to initiations in the strict sense of the word. By virtue of these ceremonies she acquires a new position within a hierarchy regulated according to religion and social status. Even in this, her very own place, she is within the domain of the triad Ceres, Liber, and Libera. She is then subject to the law of Ceres.

Does a real wedding actually take place here? As in Bruegel's *Country Wedding,* the bridegroom is missing. The question deserves serious consideration in a monument such as the frieze of the mysteries which seems to exclude men on principle. Moreover, thesmophoric secret rituals may have been maturity rites in origin, a theory which has gained probability with regard to Attic *arrephorai.*[100] In that aspect the god Liber is also included if only for the male part of society. On the day of the Liberalia, March 17, a boy received his man's toga.[101] In the frieze in Pompeii the Bacchic element prevails. But the initiation—or initiations—into an exclusive cult was obviously also meant here, perhaps, even in preparation for a wedding, even though nothing is known about this, nor why *virgines* participated in the nocturnal ceremony of the *anniversarium.* Various possible explanations could still be considered. It is not impossible that the bridal scenes were to point out the contrast to the Bacchic world of maenads in a manner similar to the representation on the Djemila mosaic which, in my opinion, shows the same contrast. The continuity of the themes then would be expressed in the interrelated contrasts rather than in the progress of the action. Thus, the action would have to include all contrasts, from the maenads experiencing only themselves to matrimonial union as the goal and highest degree of fulfillment.

To consider that the *ordo matronarum* received a new member with every appropriate wedding seems to me especially important since this fact establishes a parallel to the Bacchic cult actions that precede the bridal scenes.[102] Our approach shows that many of the rites and actions under scrutiny can be interpreted in multiple ways. In a certain sense, they are all "rites de passage" designed to transfer human beings from one station in life to another. Wedding rites are intended to detach the bride from her original family and to admit her to a new one. Mystical initiations transfer human beings into a new religious frame of mind and, at the same time, award them a new and higher religious degree. Then, initiation and admission become the same, and in this sense—aside from other possible interpretations—mystical initiations and weddings are indeed comparable. If the word initiation is really valid for the frieze, then it means, among other things, admission to a new social class in the form of a cult association whose full members held the rank of matron and which traditionally emphasized the sacral autonomy of the women's society. Normally, the young girl becomes a matron by marriage; through the mysteries she gains a religious position. From this point of view a similarity between the maenad and the bride of the frieze exists, notwithstanding all the contrasts. They can be considered as equals, all the more since the word matron seems to have been used also as an independent title unrestrained by factual marriage.[103] As long as the transition from maenad to matron in the frieze of the mysteries cannot be differently and more convincingly supported by ancient evidence, it seems advisable to consider also the analogical data which may have connected these seemingly contradictory forms of life.

In spite of everything, it is not impossible that another solution could still be found, that is, an interpretation demonstrating a direct development from the maenads to the bridal scenes. I would like to recall here once more the above-mentioned episode of Amata in Vergil's *Aeneid*. There the girl Lavinia, before she can become a bride, is abducted into the woods by a swarm of Latinian maenads and offered by her own mother to the lord of the Bacchic turmoil. J. Gagé has pointed out the possibility that this idea may easily go back to a cult practice that once existed. For the present it is only an hypothesis, but if this or a similar suggestion holds, the result would indeed be a sequence of events which corresponds exactly to the pictorial order of the frieze. At least in Vergil's story the identification with the maenads would be equal to what we would have to recognize in the frieze: a preparatory experience, followed by the wedding.[104] The question about the meaning of the bridal scenes and their place in relation to the whole can now be asked in the following manner. Do we have to view the allusions to wedding and marriage as the result of the preceding actions, that is, as their goal and end, or is it rather the opposite? Is the position of a matron the prerequisite for admission into the cult group and participation in its mysteries? For the time being, I would like to leave the question unanswered, exactly because both answers are possible. In both interpretations the frieze is closely drawn together as a whole; if there are any joints, they are not immediately visible. Thus, let us look once more at the *Domina* who concludes the frieze. The young woman in the dressing scene preceding her is definitely a bride. Perhaps both are the same person. In any case the *Domina* waiting on the *kline* is *nova nupta* and therefore already a matron; however, the place and particular moment might suggest that she is principally a titular matron.

Notes

*It would not be possible to cite the entire literature, which has been accumulating since 1910, regarding every detail of the frieze that will be discussed in the following essay. In most cases this would have meant a repetition of well-known opinions. Instead, we are fortunate enough to be able to refer to two recent papers containing critical summaries of earlier research; these constitute the basis for further investigation. The first includes a brief annotated bibliography, chronologically arranged, almost up to the year of its publication: R. Herbig, *Neue Beobachtungen am Fries der Mysterien-Villa in Pompeji* (1958) bibliography 70ff (hereafter: Herbig, *Beobachtungen*). The second is F. Matz's Διονυσιακὴ Τελετή, AbhMainz (1963), which includes publications after 1957 (hereafter: Matz, *Telete*). For earlier literature, see these two papers.

Special attention should be given to two inquiries which have proved to be basic for the discussion of the entire frieze: M. Bieber, *JdI* 43 (1928) 298ff. and L. Curtius, *Die Wandmalerei Pompejis* (1929) 343ff. Note also that in the same year J. Toynbee in *JRS* 19 (1929) 67ff proposed an interpretation with results very similar to those of Bieber. In order to relieve the footnotes of superfluous repetitions, current dictionaries, like W. H. Roscher, *MythLex* and *RE*, are cited only for special reasons. For the present subject, see especially the following articles in *RE*: XIII 1, 538ff., s.v. "Liknon" (W. Kroll 1926); XVI 2, esp. 1290ff., s.v. "Mysterien" (O. Kern 1935); XIX 2, esp. 1701ff., 1712ff., s.v. "Phallos" (H. Herter 1938).

It is not necessary to mention in every case whether or not the author agrees with the opinions of others.

1. The room perhaps should not be called a hall; in any case, it is a modest one. The floor space measures 7 x 5 m.: Herbig, *Beobachtungen* 7.
2. Herbig, *Beobachtungen* 10ff.
3. Similarly Herbig, *Beobachtungen* 65: "whitish-yellow"; in addition, lilac-colored vertical stripes. On the white clothing of the initiated in Eleusis: *RE* XVI 2, 1237, s.v. "Mysterien." This rule for clothes perhaps first came into use in Roman times: Pringsheim in *RE, op. cit.*
4. Horace, *Carmina* I.1. 29ff.
5. Herbig, *Beobachtungen* 33f., 74; also see infra n. 6.
6. A. Vogliano and F. Cumont, *AJA* 37 (1933) 215ff., inscription from Tusculum.
7. Cumont, *ibid.* 265ff. Matz, *Telete* 48ff. The costume thus named consisted of a mantle twisted (knotted?) around the hip. For etymology, cf. Plutarch, *Pyrrhus* 27. 3; also Euripides, *Bacchae* 698.
8. Basic is H. Usener, *RömMitt* 57 (1902) 177ff. Cf. K. Wyss, *RVV* XV 2 (*Die Milch bei den Griechen und Römern*) and infra n. 92. Villa Medici sarcophagus: Matz, *Telete* pl. 22. A mixture is certainly concocted here in a crater; with what is not clear. Wine can hardly have been lacking, in conformity with the customary use of the crater.
9. The action being performed here certainly cannot be explained with the formula "to take and to replace" of the Eleusinian mysteries. These involve very different ideas and symbols; see now M. Mehauden, *Le Sécret Central de l'Initiation aux Mystères d'Eleusis*, ed. C. J. Bleeker (1965) 67ff., with bibliography.
10. Examples in E. Winternitz, *MittKhInstFlorenz* II (1965) 277ff., esp. 279.
11. Vergil, *Ecl.* VI.27ff.
12. Music inspires *enthusiasmos*; it is the means, not the consequence, of divine frenzy, and in this respect comparable to wine: Aristotle, *Pol.* VIII.5. 16; 7. 4.
13. Herbig, *Beobachtungen* 30ff. He, like Bieber, *JdI* 43 (1928) 304, calls the girl "Paniske." The representation is unique, although it plays with traditional conceptions: maenads suckle kids in Euripides, *Bacchae* 700. On an Etruscan tombstone from Tarquinia (London, Brit. Mus. D 22), a Bacchic initiate, perhaps a priestess, offers a drink from her kantharos to a fawn: F. Messerschmidt, *SteMat* 5 (1928) 26, pl. 4.
14. Like Daphnis and Chloe in Longos's novel. This literary comparison concerns only the milieu: the pictorial reflection of pastoral life. It does not presume the mystical interpretation of the ancient novel as recommended by R. Merkelbach, *Roman und Mysterium* (1962), which needs further examination; Matz: *Telete* 6. However, one mystical aspect of the novel should be mentioned which is of special interest here; namely, the significance Longos places on pastoral music. The shepherds Daphnis and Chloe seem to be human duplicates of Pan and Syrinx: H. Chalk, *JHS* 80 (1960) 37; also supra n. 13.
15. *Ecl.* VI.13ff.; the bucolic idyl forms the frame. The cosmic song follows: the revealing of the secrets of nature by the inspired sage, 31–40. Only then do the mythical stories come, the subjects of the narrative art, 41ff.
16. The unfavorable rating of the flute started in classical times, after the middle of the fifth century B.C. The sources seem to have been primarily Athenian intellectuals and performing musicians (Melanippos), as well as advocates of a new "ethical" music theory: Plato, *Rep.* III.399.C–D. Here we can but note the long aftereffect of this classical opposition between a "higher" and a "lower" kind of music in neo-Platonic theory and, branching out from there, in Renaissance philosophy. In Roman pastoral poetry the reed pipe is *agrestis*: Vergil, *Ecl.* VI.8. On the other hand, we must remember that the various types of flute, especially the aulos, were generally considered as instruments of Dionysiac music, in contrast to the Apollonian cithara. In this respect too, the lyre-playing Silenus is a remarkable but still problematic figure. For the recently discovered Cybele from Bogazköy whose little companions play the aulos as well as a stringed instrument, see K. Bittel in *Antike Plastik* II (1963) 7ff., esp. 20f.
17. Examples in Herbig, *Beobachtungen* figs. 35, 36; Matz, *Telete* 22f. The expressive motive of a female figure grasping her mantle as a sign of fright can already be found in early classical painting;

cf. the frightened Gaia on the Tityos cup by the Penthesilea Painter in Munich: G. Neumann, *Gesten und Gebärden in der Griechischen Kunst* (1965) 41, figs. 18, 178, n. 127.

18. Bieber, *JdI* 43 (1928) 304; similarly, *idem, The Review of Religion* 2 (1937) 8: "The horror is not only injected by the huge symbol, but by the sinister winged figure . . ." Likewise, Herbig, *Beobachtungen* 29.

19. Especially Curtius, *Wandmalerei Pompejis* 363.

20. Curtius was the main exponent of the theory of copies, *ibid*. 362ff.; cf. Herbig, *Beobachtungen* 73.

21. Also Matz, *Telete* 27.

22. Black-figure pitcher, unpublished, privately owned in Basel. I wish to thank the owner, R. Hess, for the photograph and information. Scene at the well: girl hurries to the right, frightened by the phallus which appears behind her above the curb of the well. The young shepherd on the Boston crater flees before Pan in the same way: J. D. Beazley, *Der Panmaler* (1931) 10, pl. 2.

23. R. Herbig, *AA* (1925) 262ff.; cf. *Beobachtungen* 15, 37, n. 1.

24. Invisibility: A. Pease, *HSCP* 53 (1942) 1ff.

25. Matz, *Telete* 16ff. Neither is the content of the liknon equally clear in all representations nor is it necessarily always the same. The liknon can contain other objects or it can be empty. See also infra n. 87.

26. The liknon is the cradle of Dionysos Liknites. The child lies in it. The celebration of the Thyiades on Parnassus and the cult in Delphi are connected with the pre-Apollonian religion, probably the old local cult of the earth goddess. M. P. Nilsson, *The Dionysiac Mysteries of the Hellenistic and Roman Age* (1957) 21ff. (hereafter: *Dionysiac Mysteries*), derives the liknon from the cult of Priapus. In doing so, he emphasizes the originally foreign nature of the liknon in the Dionysiac arsenal, although the derivation from Priapus can hardly explain the situation; cf. F. Matz, *Gnomon* 32 (1960) 534ff. An early example of the connection of liknon, phallus, and Dionysus appears on an Apulian crater in Trieste: E. Simon, *JdI* 76 (1961) 171, fig. 37. Earth goddess and liknon of the child Dionysus: M. P. Nilsson, *Geschichte der griechischen Religion* I (1941) 546f.; *idem, Dionysiac Mysteries* 38ff.

27. Phallic rites and symbols in the cult of Demeter: *RE* XIX 2, 1712ff., s.v. "Phallos"; see also infra n. 94.

28. Many monuments from early classical times on show the frequently represented maenads resisting satyrs: Nilsson, *Dionysiac Mysteries* 567f.; M. E. Edwards, *JHS* 80 (1960) 78f., with older literature. Cf. esp. A. Rapp, *RömMitt* 27 (1872) 695f. concerning the maenads' hostility to men and marriage. In the early sixth century it was still different; on monuments of this time satyrs and their nymphs—who hardly differ from the maenads—get on much better together. Cf. the erotic scene on the Phineus cup in Würzburg: E. Langlotz, *Griechische Vasen im M. von Wagner-Museum* (1932) 23ff.

29. H. von Rohden and H. Winnefeld, *Architektonische römische Tonreliefs* I 52ff., pl. 123. M. Bieber, *JdI* 43 (1928) 309. Later suggestions for interpretation, with literature, Matz, *Telete* 27, 8 no. 5.

30. The cult is verified in literature. There seem to have been pictures also, but the iconography is uncertain: G. Bermond Montanari in *EAA* I (1958) 171, s.v. "Aidos."

31. E. Simon, *JdI* 76 (1961) 136f. The starting point for this interpretation, the explanation of the winged figure with the spike of grain on the Telephos picture in Naples as the constellation Virgo, has not yet been proven. It is a problem by itself, which unfortunately cannot be treated here. For the literature, *ibid*. 138 n. 4. Cf. Matz, *Gnomon* 32 (1960) 545, and *Telete* 7, 27f.

32. FR pl. 47. J. D. Beazley, *ARV²* (1963) 370, 12. The proper contrast must be sought with the gods themselves. Iris acts only on behalf of Hera, who gets herself into danger on the other side of the same cup: F. Brommer, *Satyrspiele²* (1959) 27f., 73, nos. 28–34b. Iris' mission, therefore, need not always be the same. On the London cup she steals parts of the offering from Dionysus' altar. There is no altar on the Campana relief, and what the unveiled liknon contained the thief did not like. Helbig related the representation on the terracotta relief to Iris, which is basically correct: *Führer durch Rom³* (1914) no. 1518 (relief in the Museo Nazionale delle Terme).

33. Mosaic from the Roman villa near Djemila-Cuicul, Algeria: Matz, *Telete* 9, no. 16, pl. 24. According to the coiffures of the women, circa first half of the third century A.D. Similarly, L. Leschi, *MonPiot* 35 (1935/36) 139ff.; probable date, early third century A.D.: *ibid*. 169; see also infra n. 52.

34. Matz, *Telete* 22.

35. Complete mosaic in Leschi, *MonPiot* 35 (1935/36) 141, fig. 1. Two of the four lateral scenes deal with the childhood and education of the little Dionysus. Ikarios sacrificing and the dancing figure next to the unveiling of the liknon fill the remaining sides, but hardly as a continuous sequence. All the pictures share only the generally Bacchic theme; this applies also for the central picture that represents the raging Lykurgos.

    Matz, *Telete* 22 correctly identified the *tabellae* held by the seated woman. What they contained remains uncertain. We would expect a ἱερὸς λόγος (Matz, *ibid.*) on a scroll. The frieze of the mysteries shows several such scrolls. The explanation as a marriage contract is supported by the similar *tabellae* on the *kline* of the waiting figure: Herbig, *Beobachtungen* 39.

36. Matz, *Telete* 31f.

37. K. Rathe, *Die Ausdrucksfunktion extrem verkürzter Figuren* (1938). Similarly graduated frontal groups occur from the middle of the second century B.C. on late Hellenistic reliefs, esp. in Lagina: A. Schober, *Der Fries des Hekateions von Lagina* (1933). In Roman art before the middle of the first century B.C., the disbandment of veterans on the Ahenobarbus base can be compared, esp. the backward action of the seated figure in the second group from the left: I. Scott-Ryberg, *Rites of the State Religion in Roman Art* (1955) fig. 17a.

38. Akratos: main evidence, Paus. I.2. 5. Interesting material in E. Gerhard, *Schmückung der Helena* 4BWPr (1845) 10. Thus, Akratos was a daemon, represented as a mask, connected with Dionysus but not identical. The name points to the still unmixed new wine; for the religious significance of the new wine, see Nilsson, *Griechische Religion* I 554f., 564, with reference to the feasts of the Anthesteria, Choes, and Pithoigiai. Consequently, the daemon Akratos must be understood as the personification of the new wine. Cf. also the Akratos mask on a round cist, the prop for a Roman statue of standing Dionysus (Rome, Vatican Museums): G. Lippold, *Vat. Kat.* III, *Gall. dei Candelabri*, no. 29. Akratos seems to be especially linked to the mask god of Choes. After all, Dionysos Akratophoros in Phigaleia, according to the description in Paus. VIII.39. 5, must have been quite similar to the mask idol on the so-called Lenaia vases. The mask of Akratos had the features of Silenus: South Italian vase from Lipari, with inscription, now in Glasgow, *JHS* 7 (1886) 55, fig. 2, pl. 62 (infra Fig. 23). In Athens Akratos was the patron of the Dionysiac *technites*, that is, the artists and particularly the musicians: E. Maass, *Jdl* 2 (1890) 102ff. The little tomb sanctuary on an Apulian vase, decorated with mask and kantharos, might be related to this conception: *CVA Lecce* (2) pl. 33, 34; the dead perhaps belonged to a sodality of Akratos. The bearded mask in a liknon worshipped by women on a libation vessel should be related, however, to Dionysus himself: G. van Hoorn, *Choes and Anthesteria* (Amsterdam, 1951) no. 271, fig. 38. Cf. also Nilsson, *Dionysiac Mysteries* 28ff., 98, fig. 24: the mask excites fear.

39. Details in Matz, *Telete* 30ff.

40. Aeschylus: κάτοπτρον εἴδους χαλκός ἐστ᾽, οἶνος δὲ νοῦ, Frag. 670 (ed. H. J. Mette). Anakreon: J. Bergk, Anacreontea 60, *Poetae Lyrici Graeci* III² (1914) 33 J.

41. DarSag, s.v. "Akratophorum." Vessels of this form appear repeatedly on monuments, but to my knowledge the examples have not been collected. It is interesting that such a vessel occurs on the Munich black-figure vase which Nilsson related to the Attic feast of Choes, the Anthesteria vase in Munich, *SBMünchen* (1930) Abh. 4, fig. I; this is how I would actually like to explain the "jug" which the standing woman on the right holds in her hand. A vessel of the same kind, only larger, is handed to the standing maenad on the left in a Pompeian painting representing the triumphal procession of the child Dionysus: Curtius, *Wandmalerei Pompejis* 298f., fig. 172; from the house of M. Lucretius Fronto, counterpart to *ibid.* 297, fig. 171.

42. Herbig, *Beobachtungen* 34f.; Matz, *Telete* 24ff.

43. The night has black wings: Aristophanes, *Aves* 695. Cf. *Mnemosyne* 7 (1939) 169.

44. Matz, *Telete* 7, 27f.

45. *Dionysiac Mysteries* 125; cited by Matz, *Telete* 23.

46. Numerous examples, esp. on Volterran ash urns: e.g., C. Laviosa, *Scultura Tardo-Etrusca di Volterra* (1964) 41, pl. 12; 69, pl. 33; 167, pl. 106. R. Herbig, *Götter und Dämonen der Etrusker* (1965) pl. 28, 2 (goddesses of death).

47. Critique in Matz, *Telete* 24f.

48. Lyssa, daughter of the Night, rouses madness in Lykurgos; representations on Apulian vases: K. Deichgräber, *NNG* 3 (1938/39) 294ff., pl. 3–5.

    To goad or to whip up human passions is a common metaphor. The tools necessary for it change. Cf. Scholion Euripides, *Hippolytos* 1194 (ed. Schwartz) regarding the exchangeability of

Fig. 23. Akratos, South Italian calyx-krater from
Lipari, Glasgow Art Gallery and Museum

Fig. 24. Dionysus as a child riding on a panther, mosaic from Roman villa near
Djemila, Algeria

κέντρον and μάστιξ; also staff and horsewhip in Hippolytos's hand: *JdI* 28 (1913) 314. The spirit is "whipped up by the Muses": P. Friedländer, *Joannes von Gaza* (1932) 166. In the same way Erotes also whip their victims: mirror box, New York, Metr. Mus. No. 765; W. Züchner, *Griechische Klappspiegel* (1942) 46f., pl. 13 (K 60). More examples can be found.

49. Herbig, *Beobachtungen* 70, 1913, pl. 34.

50. Euripides, *Bacchae* 862f.: the Dionysiac ecstasy means rescue and protection.

51. Supra n. 48. The Latin counterpart of the Greek Lyssa is of special interest here, the description of Alecto and her influence on the unfortunate queen Amata: Vergil, *Aen.* VII.378ff. The fury Alecto is also a daughter of the Night with dark wings, *ibid.* 331. She turns Amata into a raging maenad, driven round like a top by the whip of playing boys, *ibid.* 405f.: "*dant animos plagae.*"

52. Dishevelled hair of the maenads: they are shown on innumerable vase paintings but also are mentioned in the literary tradition. Cf. Ovid, *Amores* I.14. 19, when the sleeping mistress is compared with a sleeping bacchant; see also infra n. 96 on Vergil, *Aen.* VII.389f. Initiation or atonement rites performed for sleeping maenads: Roman oscillum in Boston, Mus. of Fine Arts, *BMFA* 38 (1940) frontispiece (here, Fig. 17; courtesy Mus. of Fine Arts, Boston). The scene has not been explained, but a Bacchic rite is obviously being carried out. Perhaps we are dealing with the lustration of the Argive women who are seized with Bacchic madness or the daughters of Proitus who were punished in a similar way: *RE* XXIII 1, 123, s.v. 'Proitides' (G. Radke); cf. the South Italian vase painting in Syracuse, *BdA* 35 (1950) 100ff. We should also ask whether the contrast between the two women in the Djemila mosaic (supra n. 33) was not based on a late version of the Proitides myth; see Apollodorus II.2. 2; III.5. 2. The good daughter is cured and marries (Melampus?), the other remains a misogamist maenad. According to the Sicyonian tradition, she is even killed like a maenad—overtaken by the pursuer while running away, Radke, *op. cit.* 124. Her name is Iphinoe, and that is what the dancer on the mosaic should be called. Unfortunately, the mythological tradition is very contradictory. It is not unlikely that the madness of the Proitides consisted precisely in their negation of marriage, but no reliable answer can be given.

53. *JbMusBern* 41/42 (1961/62) figs. 1, 8. I would prefer to call the winged figure on these coins and on the cameo in Copenhagen simply Nike, which amounts to a good Hellenistic meaning, but there is not enough room here to substantiate this suggestion. Her blow is probably expected to wake up the sleeper, to incite him to new deeds. The instrument of percussion changes; in fig. 8 it is, in my opinion, a scepter whose shaft has been drawn bent only by accident. That explains the pommel at the upper end. Cf. "Observations on the Allegory of the Pompeian Death's-Head Mosaic" in this volume, 11ff. Figs. 1, 4: the Roman-Hellenistic form of the scepter as symbol of sovereignty.

54. I owe the oral reference to this likely association to W. Burkert. The later, allegorical interpretation of ecstasy as sleep might go back to it: Philo, *Leg. Allegor.* II.9. Above all, this explains the Eleusinian order according to which the mystes must cast his eyes down: *Hom. Hymn. Demeter* 194.

55. Veiling the head, the initiate turning away, and similar measures of "not seeing" in Bacchic rites: Matz, *Telete* 16ff., esp. 18f.

56. *Beobachtungen* 47ff. Note also that the nude maenad was not a frequent figure type, especially not a classical one. Relatively early examples do appear on Italic monuments from Magna Graecia, for instance, Apulian vases around the middle of the fourth century B.C.: A. Campidoglu, *Apulian Red-figure Vase Painters of the Plain Style* (1961) pl. 23, 109, 110; Simon, *JdI* 76 (1961) 136, n. 67.

57. Most interpreters agree on that. For different opinions, cf. Simon, *ibid.* 126, 169.

58. Also Matz, *Telete* 31.

59. Bieber, *JdI* 43 (1928) 313f. More recently, B. Schweitzer, *Mythische Hochzeiten*, *SBHeidelberg* (1961) Abh. 6.

60. M. Bieber, *The Review of Religion* 2 (1937) 9.

61. Herbig, *Beobachtungen* 38; Pothos: W. Müller, *JdI* 58 (1943) 154ff.

62. The search for a better explanation would probably have to start with the Platonic theory of love; particularly *Phaedrus* 255.D 5: the loved one beholds himself in the lover "as in a mirror." Thus love and mirror symbolism have been easily joined together in the pictorial tradition since the late fifth century B.C., as, for instance, on the beautiful bronze hydria attachment representing Eros and Psyche: W. Züchner, *Griechische Klappspiegel* 178f., fig. 87; once Berlin, Staatl. Mus., now lost: A. Greifenhagen *AA* (1960) 130, fig. 81. The intellectual as well as the pictorial tradition of

these topical conceptions survived for a long time, into late antiquity, the Renaissance, and beyond. This material needs special discussion. In addition, I mention here only the "mirror of Dionysus" in which the soul perceives her own image; the metaphor, not yet fully explained, occurs in Plotinus, *Enn.* IV.3. 12.

63. Herbig, *Beobachtungen* 39. The *kline*, with only one third of its actual length shown, occurs on an onos from Eretria: M. Bieber, *JdI* 42 (1927) 315, fig. 12.

64. Bieber, *JdI* 43 (1928) 315. Aldobrandini Wedding: B. Andreae, *RömQ* 57 (1962) 3ff.

65. Ring on fourth finger of the left hand signifies bride or wedding: evidence in Bieber, *JdI* 43 (1928) 312, n. 5. On the wedding contract, see *ibid.* 329. Along with Herbig (*Beobachtungen* 39), I identify it with the *tabellae*—closed diptychon—on the *kline* next to the waiting woman. Herbig's suggestion that she does not represent the bride but the mother contradicts all ancient wedding pictures known to us; moreover, the accumulation of the wedding symbols around her, including the bridal bed, make it unlikely that the waiting figure is not the legitimate owner of these things. The yellow veil, here with a purple seam, also belongs to the bride according to Roman custom: A. Crowfoot, *BSA* 37 (1936/37) 40, n. 6.

66. Curtius, *Wandmalerei Pompejis* 361f. Also Nilsson, *Dionysiac Mysteries* 66ff., esp. 74.

67. Change of clothes for symbolic purposes in later mystery religions, especially of Isis: *RE* XVI 2, 1929f., s.v. "Mysterien."

68. The Athenian month *Gamelion*, in which the Dionysiac feast of Lenaia fell, was named for the institutional protectress of marriage, Hera Gamelia. It cannot be generally designated as a wedding month. Neither can any communal weddings in this month be cited nor were there any initiations of brides: M. P. Nilsson, "Wedding Rites in Ancient Greece, Opuscula Selecta" III (1960) 243f. Connections with Dionysus arise from the season. The wine which was pressed out in early fall could be considered as fully fermented in February: Plutarch, *Q. Conv.* III.7. 1. The Dionysiac festivals of the Anthesteria follow a little later (supra n. 38). Not much can be stated with certainty about the Lenaia themselves: Nilsson, "Griechische Religion" I 551, 559, n. 2.

69. M. Bieber, "Eros and Dionysus on Kerch Vases," *Hesperia Suppl.* 8 (1949) 31ff. For the New York libation pitcher and its explanation, see "Procession Personified" in this volume, 1–6: the "sacred wedding" at first was a ritual. Still, vase paintings of the fourth century B.C. show a tendency to attribute to it a more human, sentimental interpretation. These pictures, however, are allegories which are only vaguely related to reality. The meeting of Dionysus and Ariadne at this period sometimes resembles a human love story and marriage; this is hardly applicable to the original character of the myth: E. Simon, *AntK* 6 (1963) 11ff.; also E. Metzger, *Recherches sur l'Imagerie Athénienne* (1965) 62ff. Cf. also Nilsson, *Dionysiac Mysteries* 66ff.; and infra n. 70.

70. The Basilinna thereby represented the city of Athens on account of her position (ὑπὲϱ τῆς πόλεως; Demosthenes, *Against Neaera* LIX.72–73, ed. W. Rennie). The cause of the Boeotian Daidala is comparable, Paus. IX.3: wedding of the city heroine Plataia with Zeus. There the "bride" was a wooden doll (Daidalon), which at the end was burned on Mt. Kithairon. The yearly wedding with Dionysus was a concern of the city, a state act, not unlike that other more famous ceremony: "Wenn der Doge von Venedig/ Mit dem Meere sich vermählt." The office of the Archon Basileus was the place assigned for it, which suggests that even at its beginning the cult was located in the royal dwelling. As to the ritual itself, the sources state only that it was secret. A procession corresponding to a wedding procession probably took place according to the monuments, but this is not documented in writing. Only this connection justifies occasional depictions of the Basilinna on vase paintings, especially in the wedding procession performed by children on the small pitcher in New York: L. Deubner, *Attische Feste* (1932) 104, pl. II, 2–4. Cf. Metzger, (supra n. 69) 63, n. 4.

Participation of the Archon Basileus is neither documented nor likely: E. Simon, *AntK* 6 (1963) 12, and n. 38. Regarding the meaning of sacred weddings generally, cf. Nilsson, *Griechische Religion* I 110ff., 554f.

71. Matz, *Telete* 5f. (Now published: *idem, Die dionysischen Sarkophage* [*Die antiken Sarkophagreliefs*], 3 vols., 1968–69.)

72. Herbig, *Beobachtungen* 22; Curtius, *Wandmalerei Pompejis* 356.

73. Esp. Curtius, *ibid.* 367ff. Early Hellenistic dating of the prototype: F. Matz, *AA* (1944) 94ff. See also infra n. 77.

74. R. Lee, "Ut Pictura Poesis," *ArtB* 22 (1940) 247ff., figs. 21–24 (now published in book form, 1967).

75. Curtius, *Wandmalerei Pompejis* 367: originally a matriarchal cult which survived in a paternalistic society. The practice is there related to the Greek Artemis.

76. For illustrations: Bieber, *JdI* 43 (1928) 301; Curtius, *Wandmalerei Pompejis* 369; Simon, *JdI* 76 (1961) 133, fig. 15. In addition, highly comparable terracottas from Myrina: R. Lullies, *MdI* I (1948) 51; Herbig, *Beobachtungen* figs. 31, 32.

77. Aristeides of Thebes: Pliny, *Nat. Hist.* XXXV.24. 100; VII.126; Strabo VIII.381; summary: W. Sauer in Thieme-Becker, s.v. The Dionysus picture was probably painted for Corinth. It survived the destruction by Mummius in 146 B.C. but was subsequently sold to Attalus III of Pergamon. From there it came to Rome, probably after 133 B.C.

78. The fact that the Dionysus picture by Aristeides was in Rome, at least for a while, increases the probability that copies of it could have been made and circulated in Italy. The original could be seen easily and was accessible to the public.

79. For the history of the Roman temple of Ceres and related questions, see: H. Le Bonniec, *Le Culte de Cérès à Rome* (1958) 254ff.; Liber identical with Dionysus-Bacchus; *ibid.* 308ff.; Libera-Ariadne: Ovid, *Fasti* III.511ff. Contradictions in the ancient interpretations of the triad Ceres, Liber, Libera: Le Bonniec, *op. cit.* 305f.

80. Cult and feasts of the triad: *ibid.* 277ff. We must remember that Liber belongs originally to Libera and that therefore the triad must read: Ceres and the couple Liber-Libera, *ibid.* 294.

81. *Ibid.* 396ff.

82. Meetings of women in the cult of a triad consisting of Demeter, Kore, Dionysus: the Nymphon in Phlius, Paus. II.11. 3. The same applies to the Attic Haloa. An initiation by a priestess is also mentioned among their ceremonies: Bieber, *JdI* 43 (1928) 315, n. 2. Literary evidence for a connection between Dionysus and Demeter is more frequent in Rome than in Greece: Le Bonniec, *op. cit.* 298. Thesmophoria: Nilsson, *Griechische Religion* I 109; Deubner, *Attische Feste* 50ff. The late Hellenistic fragments of a frieze that is now partly in Athens and partly in Würzburg could also be of interest here. Perhaps they represent a thesmophoria procession from Asia Minor, possibly from Halicarnassus, third quarter of the second century, H. Möbius, *AM* 77 (1962) 282ff.

83. Regarding these institutions here and in the following: J. Gagé, *Matronalia* (Ed. Latomus LX, 1963) esp. Ch. II, 100ff.

84. Fortunae: *ibid.* 12ff.; cf. also Brendel, *AJA* 64 (1960) 41ff. Mater Matuta: Gagé, *op. cit.* 159. Bona Dea: *ibid.* 137.

85. Le Bonniec, *op. cit.* 424ff.; also Gagé, *op. cit.* 140f.

86. Main source is Livy XXXIX.8ff. Mitigating modifications are mentioned on the bronze tablet from Tiriolo: O. Elia, *RömMitt* 69 (1962) 124f., nn. 19, 20. The Senate's objection is directed on principle against the participation of men; this seems to have been the chief reason for the prohibition: Cicero, *De Leg.* II.35–37. Moreover, Nilsson, *Dionysiac Mysteries* 14ff.

87. Matz, *Telete* 33f. Locrian reliefs: È. Langlotz, *Ancient Greek Sculpture in South Italy and Sicily,* no. 71ff. (with literature); K. Schauenburg, *JdI* 68 (1953) 38ff. Underworld connections of the bearded Dionysus on late classical, Hellenistic, and Roman monuments: A. Bruhl, *Liber Pater* (1953) 309ff. The important volute crater in the Museo Archeologico in Ferrara, attributed to the Polygnotos Painter and discovered in 1923 at Spina, should be mentioned here too. Best illustrations in S. Aurigemma, *La Necropoli di Spina in Valle Trebbia* I 1 (1960) 48ff., pls. 19–30; earlier literature, *ibid.* and P. E. Arias, *ArchCl* 10 (1958) 21ff. Dionysus and a companion are enthroned in a cult building in order to receive a festival procession which approaches from the right and seems to move around the whole vessel; both deities hold a scepter and libation cups similar to those of the enthroned deities of the Locrian relief. There can hardly be any doubt that it is Dionysus who is represented, but the supposition that he takes the place of Hades as god of the netherworld remains quite uncertain. His crowned *paredros* is without name. Her identification as Chloe is based on an erroneous reading: Arias, *op. cit.* 21ff. She lets a small lion play on her shoulder and left arm as if it were a domestic cat. This might be a maenadic element; she is the princess of the thiasos, in this case most likely Ariadne. The procession is led by a white-haired priestess who carries a veiled liknon on her head; behind her, a flute-playing girl, then two orgiastic dancers and two aulists; underneath, children and two men. The women, however, are in the majority. The liknon appears here for the first time in a Bacchic ritual; the vase is to be dated around 440 B.C. Unfortunately, nothing can be said about the contents of the liknon because it is covered with a cloth. Next to the priestess is a sacrificial altar with logs. We must assume that the contents of the liknon were designed as the sacrifice on this altar. A definite feast is certainly meant. In contrast to the Locrian reliefs where Hades, Persephone, and Dionysus are clearly recognizable in a close cult relationship, nothing points to relations to underworld deities.

88. Similarly, Le Bonniec, *op. cit.* 306: "La triade renferme donc plus d'un germe de dissolution." The foundation of the temple in 493 B.C. gave the triad its official form. Ideas tending in this direction must have preceded the final formalization of the cult, *ibid.* 304.

89. The *sacrum* is first documented for the year 216 B.C. It was obviously a Hellenistic reorganization from among the Roman cults, Le Bonniec, *op. cit.* 400ff., and thus different from the older Cerealia. The celebration was supervised by Greek priestesses, called probably from Campania, *ibid.* 396ff. These enjoyed high social prestige, *ibid.* 399.

90. *Orci nuptiae:* Le Bonniec, *op. cit.* 438ff. Discovery of Proserpina: *ibid.* 412ff. Even so, the tendency of the entire celebration was not Eleusinian, as far as we know. Only the exclusiveness of the ritual, the categorical limitation to female participants, gives it a thesmophoric character. In this too I follow Le Bonniec, *ibid.* 420f.

91. Servius in *Aen.* IV.58. Cf. Le Bonniec, *op cit.* 421; Gagé, *Matronalia* 143f.

92. Gagé, *Matronalia* 139, n. 2. Wine was permitted in this celebration but it was not to be mentioned; it was circumscribed with other words, the vessel containing the wine called *mellarium*, the contents called milk: Macrobius, *Sat.* I.12. 25. Also in Greece Demeter generally maintains a reserved attitude toward the Dionysiac drink; for instance, she refuses wine in her sorrow: *Hom. Hymn. Demeter* 206f. The refusal of food and drink is certainly a general and natural expression of mourning. From this it does not necessarily follow that the denial of certain food and beverages cannot also assume special meanings. Demeter's refusal of wine complies with the restriction to the *nephalia*—libations excluding wine—in the cult. Both in themselves presume by definition an opposition to the god of wine.

93. Detailed discussion of the sources, Le Bonniec, *op. cit.* 404ff. It is possible but not certain that in this preparatory period of abstinence the consumption of bread was prohibited. That could be understood as ritual imitation of the Eleusinian myth. The myth itself represents an agrarian logic: the "mourning" field lacks fruits, the bread is not there. The sources, however, are hardly sufficient to make the abstention from bread for the Roman *castum Cereris* more than probable at best.

94. Deubner has similarly concluded that in the procession of the Attic, so-called rustic Dionysia, basket and phallus represented an older religious phase upon which were superimposed the Dionysiac symbols of wine amphora and vine: *Attische Feste* 136. The lack of homogeneity in the cults in the Roman temple of Ceres has rightly been emphasized by Le Bonniec: the mysteries of the *anniversarium* with their thesmophoric character refer only to Ceres and the recovered daughter. Liber and Libera are not considered, they are not mentioned. The complete triad of deities did not participate at any celebration of mysteries: Le Bonniec, *op. cit.* 438.

95. Supra n. 33.

96. Supra n. 89. In this connection, we have to refer once more to the Amata episode, Vergil, *Aen.* VII. esp. 389ff.: "*euhoe Bacche fremens, solum te virgine dignum. . . .*" It becomes obvious that Amata would prefer that her daughter be dedicated to Bacchus—most likely as a maenad—in order to avoid her hateful marriage with Aeneas. Yet here too a concept of marriage plays a part, although its kind is unworldly. "You alone worthy of the virgin"—does this not postulate the god as mystic spouse? Cf. Philostratus, *Imag.* II.17. 9: the bacchant turns away from Silenus; 'The striking picture of Dionysus whom she loves is before her soul . . .' W. Otto, *Dionysos* (1933) 161.

97. A. Maiuri, *La Villa dei Misteri* (1931) I 223ff., figs. 93–98.

98. M. Della Corte, *RendNap* 24/25 (1949/50) 101ff.

99. Thus the thyrsos is ready for the Dionysus child as proof of his later power. Zeus—the father—holds it in his left hand on the crater by the Altamura Painter while with his right he supports the boy who stands on his knee; certainly he holds it not as his own attribute but in order to hand it over to the child later, or perhaps to the assisting nymphs: H. Fuhrmann, *JdI* 65/66 (1950/51) 118ff. On the Djemila mosaic (Fig. 24), a nymph takes the child by the hand that already holds the thyrsos. At the same time, the child learns to ride on the panther: the education of Dionysus, *MonPiot* 35 (1935/36) pl. 8. The sarcophagus in Princeton which was discussed by E. Simon also contains a similar scene in which a *narthex* takes the place of the thyrsos: *RömMitt* 69 (1962) 141f., pl. 45, 2.

100. W. Burkert, *Hermes* 94 (1966) 1ff.

101. Ovid, *Fasti* III.771ff.

102. Gagé, *Matronalia* 126ff.; for the Roman characteristics of this institution, *ibid.* 100ff.

103. *Ibid.* 224; until now only late evidence: Isid. Sev., *Origines* I.573.

104. Gagé, *Matronalia* 235ff.; 238 with reference to the old celebration of the Liberalia in Lavinium.

Index